D0898155

FROM HOLOCAUST TO HARVARD

Also by
JOHN G. STOESSINGER

The Refugee and the World Community
The Might of Nations: World Politics in Our Time
Financing the United Nations System
Power and Order
The United Nations and the Superpowers
Nations in Darkness: China, Russia, and America
Why Nations Go to War
Henry Kissinger: The Anguish of Power
Night Journey
Crusaders and Pragmatists: Movers of Modern American
Foreign Policy

FROM HOLOCAUST
TO HARVARD

A STORY OF ESCAPE, FORGIVENESS, AND FREEDOM

JOHN G. STOESSINGER

Skyhorse Publishing

Skyhorse Publishing books may be purchased in bulk at special discounts for sales promotion, corporate gifts, fund-raising, or educational purposes. Special editions can also be created to specifications. For details, contact the Special Sales Department, Skyhorse Publishing, 307 West 36th Street, 11th Floor, New York, NY 10018 or info@skyhorsepublishing.com.

Skyhorse® and Skyhorse Publishing® are registered trademarks of Skyhorse Publishing, Inc.®, a Delaware corporation.

Visit our website at www.skyhorsepublishing.com.

10 9 8 7 6 5 4 3 2 1

Library of Congress Cataloging-in-Publication Data is available on file.

Cover design by Richard Rossiter

Cover photo credit ThinkStock

Print ISBN: 978-1-62914-652-2
Ebook ISBN: 978-1-62914-959-2

Printed in the United States of America

CONTENTS

For Janis, with love

CHAPTER 1

Vienna, 1938

A holiday had been declared all over Austria and the schools had been closed. Tens of thousands of Viennese had dressed in their Sunday best, each straining toward the Ringstrasse. The mood in the city was festive, with church bells tolling incessantly and houses everywhere adorned with spring flowers and large swastika flags. The city had turned out en masse to greet its new Fuehrer.

The Ringstrasse—the main thoroughfare of Vienna—was a great boulevard circling the city. It seemed that all of Vienna was lining "the Ring" to celebrate Austria's absorption into the Reich; it was the day of the Anschluss, and Adolf Hitler was making his triumphal entry into Vienna in a grand motorcade several miles long. He was to be welcomed by the blaring of trumpets and the thunder of drums from scores of marching bands, accompanied by the marching of the vast goose-stepping armies of the Wehrmacht, the SS, and the SA. The German leader was to ride past the waving throngs of Viennese in an open limousine.

By the time I arrived, the crowd lining the Ringstrasse had already begun to cheer, even before the Fuehrer's arrival. Latecomers, hearing the noise and fearful of missing the parade, were all running in the same direction—the young couples, eyes laughing and arms intertwined, easily overtaking the older generations.

Only ten years old and wiry, I ran faster than most. I, too, was eager to get a glimpse of the German Fuehrer who was coming to annex my hometown. Lisl had promised she would wait for me at the Beethoven statue. She was a music student at the Vienna Academy of Art my mother had hired as a part-time governess and piano teacher. Only twenty-three, Catholic, and very beautiful, her eyes were the color of cornflowers and her blond hair reached down almost to her waist. She had told me about Schubert's early death at thirty-one, and together we had made the pilgrimage to Heiligenstadt to pay homage to Beethoven. Her favorite composer was Mozart, however. Once, she had taken me to St. Stephen's Cathedral to hear the Great Mass in C Minor.

"When the angels are on duty in heaven," Lisl had said, "they play Bach; but off duty, they play Mozart."

She had wept afterward when she told me that Mozart was buried in an unknown grave. I had promised her someday I would try to find Mozart's final resting place; I was so in love with Lisl, I would have promised anything to stop her tears.

But on this day, I could not spot her. By now, people were packed ten deep along the Ringstrasse, all eyes riveted on the steel-helmeted storm troopers on motorcycles who formed the vanguard of Hitler's victory procession. Soon, a row of cars appeared and the shouting became louder. I made my way through the crowd as I searched for Lisl.

"The Fuehrer will pass here in five minutes," a high-pitched voice exclaimed behind me. Turning, I saw Lisl standing in the front row and happily pushed through the last few feet of the cheering throng, finally reaching for her hand.

Lisl glanced down at me. I had never seen her look so radiant, yet she seemed strangely distant and did not give my hand the reassuring squeeze of recognition I craved. I became uneasy.

"We must be silent," she whispered, almost reverently. "The Fuehrer's car is coming."

I nodded obediently, studying Lisl's face. Her eyes seemed to burn with an ardent fire, and her hair was windblown in the March breeze. At that very moment, a great roar went through the crowd. An open Mercedes-Benz automobile had become visible in the distance and was slowly moving toward us. A solitary figure stood within it, his arm outstretched in a stiff salute.

Lisl let go of my hand and reached for the little golden cross she wore between her breasts. This was a gesture she made habitually when reciting the Lord's Prayer to me at bedtime. "It's a prayer Jews can say, too," she liked to say on those occasions.

Hitler's car was inching closer, and then, for some unknown reason, it came to a complete standstill almost directly in front of us, only a few feet away. The cheering around us had risen to a deafening crescendo: "We thank our Fuehrer. We thank our Fuehrer." Again and again the crowd chanted the same refrain. I looked at Lisl, still clutching her cross. Her eyes had become glazed.

"Holy Maria, Mother of God," she whispered. "He is the new Messiah."

Hitler had dropped his arm for a moment and stood smiling, looking handsome and kind. It seemed to me he was looking directly at Lisl. With a sudden pang of familiarity, I fixed my eyes on his mustache. *Just like Papa's,* I thought.

My beloved father, who had disappeared years ago, used to tickle the soles of my feet with his mustache as he kissed them. I was heartbroken when he vanished and had spent weeks searching for him. Convinced it was my fault he had gone away, I had promised Mama that I would never be bad again.

"Please make him come back, Mutti," I pleaded, to which my mother could only cry.

One day, I thought I saw him on the street and ran into an oncoming car. The driver had braked at the last instant; I escaped with only a few bruises.

"For a big boy of ten, you shouldn't be so careless," the doctor had warned me.

Nevertheless, I thought I saw Papa everywhere. The pain was like a wild animal raging inside me. Gradually, its grip lessened, but never left entirely. Papa's sudden disappearance would remain a mystery throughout my life.

I was awakened from my reverie by Lisl's voice, just as Hitler's car lurched forward.

"He has the most beautiful eyes," she said. "Did you notice?"

I hadn't noticed. I had been thinking about Papa. "Will Hitler be my Fuehrer, too?" I asked.

Lisl's face became grave as she placed her hand gently on my head and ran her fingers through my curls.

"I don't think so," she replied. "Hitler does not want to be the Fuehrer of the Jews." Then she took me home, through the Stadtpark and the festive crowd. I can still remember the heavy ironwork bars on the front door to our apartment house at 35 Reisnerstrasse.

"Mutti, you are part Aryan, aren't you?" I asked my mother during lunch after Lisl and I had returned home. My mother had blond hair and blue eyes, fitting the description of the ideal Aryan I had heard about in school.

"No, I am not," she answered. "I am Jewish, and so are you."

"One hundred percent?" I asked.

Mama nodded.

"Well, I don't want to be Jewish any longer," I blurted out.

The day before, I had been beaten up by some of my classmates who, only a few weeks earlier, had made it a daily practice to copy my homework. Now all the boys in school, except for a handful of Jews, were Hitler Youth, and everything had changed, even the clothes. The Hitler Youth proudly wore their new uniforms with the swastika armbands, the shining belt buckles, and the glittering daggers that bore the inscription ALLES FÜR DEUTSCHLAND. I was tired of being an outsider and the only Jew in the class.

"Why does Hitler say that everything is the fault of the Jews?" I asked my mother.

"Yes, the Jews and the bicyclists," Mama answered.

I was surprised by her response.

"Why the bicyclists?" I continued.

"Why the Jews?" retorted my mother with a small, sad smile.

I looked at her and then at Lisl, waiting for an explanation, but neither offered one. I was confused, and Mama seemed lost in thought. Lisl looked at her and then at me but did not smile.

"Come, let's go for a walk," Mama said finally, and rose from the table.

My mother was a beautiful woman who was proud of her resemblance to Marlene Dietrich. She was out much of the time, and I was always left in the care of both Lisl and Emma, the elderly cook.

"Where have you been?" I would ask my mother when she would return in the evenings.

"Shopping," Mama would say with an easy laugh, pulling me toward her. She would shower me with kisses and endearments but, after a few minutes, she would become impatient.

"Emma!" she'd call into the kitchen. "Is dinner ready?"

After dinner, Mama would usually go out for the evening, but sometimes she sat down at the piano and sang the latest Viennese hits. Once in a while, she would take me to a concert or a play at the Burgtheater, the oldest and most beautiful theater in Vienna. I cherished those brief moments in the company of my mother. Men, I noticed, would kiss her hand and look at her with admiration.

"Meet my little prince," she would say, and a strange man's hand would pat my head perfunctorily.

Sometimes she would be gone for days at a time. I never found out what Mama bought on those shopping trips since she rarely brought anything home. All I knew was that I hated those long absences—I would sulk in my room while Lisl and Emma did their best to comfort me. I would listen for Mama's footsteps when she returned for dinner.

"How's the little prince?" she would ask as Emma opened the door.

"He's been waiting for you," the cook would answer in a tone of mild reproach. "I just fixed his favorite dessert."

"I'll have some, too," my mother would say, and then she would smile at me.

During dinner, my mother would quiz me on my homework. Her questions were always easy.

"My clever little prince," she would say proudly with a laugh. "You'll be a king yet, or at least a prime minister."

Now, as we walked through the Stadtpark, Mama was serious. Swastika flags fluttered everywhere: from the park trees, its fountains and war memorials, its statues of generals, artists, and composers. Someone had even stuck one in the hand of the Schubert statue. The composer's cherubic face looked impassively into the distance while a pigeon, settled incongruously on his head, relieved itself.

"That's how Vienna treats its geniuses," my mother said sadly.

I thought of the "Unfinished Symphony," which I had heard for the first time a month before. Its insistent yearning had stirred me deeply and had prompted me to dream of Papa again. The dream was always the same: I followed him into dark tunnels and alleys, but just when I thought I could touch him, he would recede into the distance. In the end, he always eluded me.

When I woke, I would lie in bed for hours, trying to recapture the image of his face, which had been so clear in the dream. With the morning light, the image would fade, leaving only the longing in its wake.

Mama and I emerged on the north side of the Stadtpark, where the streets were narrow and paved with cobblestones. Mama, who had been silent for a while now, turned to me suddenly.

"We must leave Vienna," she said with an effort. "I am taking the train for Prague tonight. Opi and Omi want us to live there and have found us an apartment. I will come back next week and take you to Prague. In the meantime, Lisl will take care of you."

I nodded happily, anticipating an escape from my schoolyard torments. An Austrian Gymnasium was a difficult place under any circumstances, but with the takeover by the Hitler Youth, the harassment and daily beatings, school had become a nightmare. I still recall how a few boys from my class ripped the buttons, the fleur-de-lis patch, and the merit badges from my Boy Scout uniform, telling me that Jews weren't fit to be scouts. Any chance to get away from all this was welcome. Moreover, the prospect of a ride on the Vienna–Prague Express exhilarated me. Prague was an exciting city, and I loved my grandparents, whom I tended to visit every summer.

"How long will we stay in Prague?" I wanted to know.

Mama did not answer.

"Will Lisl come along?"

"No," my mother said. A sense of foreboding rose within me. I began to understand that this train ride to Prague would not be a routine vacation.

"Let's get an éclair," said Mama. She and I sometimes wandered around Vienna on Sundays, and she made it a habit to take me to her favorite pastry shop on the north side of the city, famous for its cream puffs and thick hot chocolate. But this was no Sunday. My foreboding deepened, but I was too frightened to ask any more questions.

We trudged up the hilly Berggasse in silence. The sun had broken through the clouds, making for a lovely afternoon with a hint of early spring. Halfway up the hill, my mother broke the silence with a small gasp.

"My God, here comes the dream doctor," she said.

I looked up to see a very old man with a beard coming toward us. He walked with short steps and held on to the arm of a younger woman.

"He will leave Vienna, too, the dream doctor," said Mama.

"Does he know what dreams mean?" I asked, fascinated.

"He has written a book about them," said Mama. "I tried to read it once but it made no sense to me. He is a famous old eccentric. His name is Dr. Sigmund Freud."

"What a wonderful name!" I exclaimed.

In school, we had sung Beethoven's chorale from the Ninth Symphony, set to Schiller's poem, "An die Freude." The words had made a deep impression on me.

"Can Dr. Freud make dreams have happy endings?" I asked, thinking of my recurrent nightmare about Papa, which always ended with the same frustration.

Mama broke into a cascade of affectionate laughter. "Maybe you should ask him yourself," she said.

We turned around, but the dream doctor and his companion were already at the bottom of the hill, well out of earshot.

Mama's mood darkened again. Something about our encounter with Dr. Freud seemed to have upset her, and our visit to the pastry shop proved to be an anticlimax. We returned home by mid-afternoon, where Lisl had already packed Mama's bags.

"Be a good boy," Mama said as she hugged me good-bye. "I will come back for you next week."

And then she was gone.

I loved my piano lessons with Lisl. We would sit side by side on the piano bench and play Mozart sonatinas for four hands. Lisl would usually let me play the easier part with the melody, the scent of her perfume completing the enchantment. Once, and quite by accident, my elbow touched her breast and an overpowering, delicious sensation coursed through my entire body. My brief encounter with her breast, which went quite unnoticed by Lisl, left me unable to concentrate. Lisl continued alone at the piano, accompanying her considerable skill with her rich alto voice as she sang Schubert's lieder. After that evening, I worshipped Lisl and would practice endless hours to try to please her.

Tonight I looked forward to an evening alone with Lisl. This would make up for the shock of Mama's announcement that we would leave Vienna soon. But during dinner, Lisl seemed preoccupied, and when I asked her to play for me, she shook her head and announced that she had to keep an appointment with a friend. Besides, she admonished, it would do me no harm if I practiced some Czerny exercises. Fearful of arousing Lisl's displeasure, I sat down at the piano. Lisl said that she would return in time to say good-night and then left the house.

I woke with a start later that evening, after Lisl had returned and tucked me into bed. I had heard voices whispering in Mama's bedroom, which was next to mine, separated only by a thick and heavy velvet curtain. The curtain had been installed the year before when I had come down with scarlet fever, and Mama would come in during the night and cool my burning forehead with ice-cold compresses. Now my first thought was of burglars, and I began to choke with fear. Then I recognized Lisl's voice, speaking in hushed whispers, laughing softly. I found it strange and was only partially reassured. I knew that Lisl's little room was on the other side of mine, and all was silent there.

For a while, I lay in bed and listened to the whispers coming from behind the curtain, even catching the sound of a man's voice. "It's all right," I then heard Lisl say. "He's asleep."

The whispering stopped and soon gave way to soft rhythmic moans that aroused my curiosity. I knew that I could look into my mother's bedroom by parting the curtain in the upper-left corner, so I slipped out of bed and crept toward it. Getting up on tiptoe and stretching to look, I could see that there, on Mama's big and comfortable bed, lay Lisl and a large, strange man. Both were completely naked, the man's clothes strewn all over the floor.

I immediately recognized the black uniform of the SS. A swastika armband and a belt with a silver buckle were visible on the chair, while a pair of black boots and a holstered revolver lay on the carpet.

"Stay a while," she said softly, then lifted her face and whispered, "give me a son for the Fuehrer." She reached for the cross between her breasts, clutched it with both hands, as if in prayer, and whispered reverently, "The new Messiah."

The man turned toward Lisl and reached for her. Suddenly, terror flooded my body, as if my guts were hungry wolves that were devouring me from within. My throat constricted and, almost unable to breathe, I staggered back to my bed and curled up. As the rhythmic moaning began, the fear howled inside me. I stuffed the bedsheets into my mouth to stifle my sobs and continued to lay there, twisted with anguish, long after I heard the SS officer leave Mama's room.

By the next morning, I had developed a raging fever. Lisl called the doctor, who prescribed alternate hot and cold baths. Mama returned from Prague at news of my illness and sat by my bedside for three days and nights while I slowly recovered. She told me the doctors had been unable to agree on a diagnosis, but they had said that it was serious. I kept silent.

The following week, we left for Prague. Lisl came to the station to say good-bye and give me a kiss on the cheek, but I felt nothing. Exhausted, I leaned back in a corner of the compartment and thought vaguely of Papa and Dr. Freud, the dream doctor. Mama cried as the whistle blew and the train began to move. I was never to see Lisl again.

CHAPTER 2

Prague, 1939

I came to love the Czech capital. My grandparents owned a shoe
store they had built near the square, a task that took more than
thirty years of hard work. Once a year, they took a week's vacation at an inexpensive nearby spa. One night, they ventured into
the local casino to try roulette. They had created a system where,
whenever grandfather bet red, grandmother would quickly place
a matching bet on black, thus ensuring they never lost. By the end
of the night, grandmother had won ten crowns from grandfather,
while the house got nothing.

To earn a little money, I would wait on customers in the shoe
store after school hours. On weekends, we would drive into the
surrounding woods where I would gather baskets of blueberries.
Unfailingly, grandmother would reward my efforts with a silver
five-crown piece. Then she would serve a tasty evening meal,
capped by those same blueberries that still bore the aroma of the
Bohemian woods.

My grandfather was the kindest of men. He had taught me
chess and even let me win occasionally. He'd told me having animals in the house made him nervous, but he bought me a little
dog anyway.

He also had a keen sense of humor. Once, a customer told an interminable story without a point and then, realizing that the punch line was missing, mumbled apologetically, "Goodness, now I have forgotten what I wanted to say."

"Never mind," grandfather said, shaking with laughter. "Say something similar."

Even school was pleasant. I quickly learned the language and made new friends, believing that I had left the Hitler Youth behind me for good. The teachers were gentle and had imagination, like my history teacher who would refer to Hitler as Louis the Thirtieth.

"Why?" one of us had asked.

"Because Louis the Fifteenth was a half-wit," Dr. Svoboda replied. We looked at him blankly. "That makes Hitler a total idiot," he explained.

Dr. Svoboda had also invented a game titled The Professor and the Idiot, which proved to be immensely educational. It was played by two pupils—one assuming the role of history professor and the other that of idiot—where the professor was to ask the idiot a question so simple that even a child would be able to answer it. It was then the idiot's task to give the wrong answer nonetheless, whereupon the professor had to "prove" that even this stupid reply was in fact correct.

A question as obvious as "How long was the Thirty Years' War?" followed by a response of "Seven years," could elicit highly creative responses from the professors. "Correct," they might say. "In those days, people did not fight at night; therefore, one half of the actual fighting time may be subtracted. In addition, there was no fighting on weekends and holidays. If one further subtracts the numerous interruptions due to truces and peace negotiations, one arrives at a precise fighting time of seven years."

In this case, the professor would be called the winner. But if he could not find a plausible explanation for the idiot's answer, the latter was declared the winner. I usually preferred the part of the idiot, as it was easier, yet it was amazing how much useful information I managed to accumulate thanks to this curious little game.

In the evenings, I often wandered the gaslit streets of the old city and along the banks of the river Moldau. Old Prague was full of ghosts, creating a benign and almost protective air. The river was spanned by dozens of bridges, each embellished with statues of saints, while in the distance and on top of a hill loomed Hradčany castle, the ancient seat of Bohemian kings. A boy of eleven could roam the city fearlessly and satiate his craving for adventure and mystery. There was, of course, another girl with whom I had promptly fallen in love but, unlike Lisl, she was my own age. Susi was the daughter of my mother's best friend, Trudy. Our mothers had met in Vienna and reunited in Prague, where they became inseparable. Both mothers doted on Susi and me, making it clear that, one day, they expected us to marry. We kissed once and wondered where the noses went. She called me Hansi and told me all her secrets, while I felt protective of her, as though I were a little man.

But the idyllic life in Prague was not to last. The atmosphere in the city was explosive, now that hundreds of German tanks were said to be on the outskirts. Mama had forbidden me to leave the house because of this. I leaned out of our third-story window in St. Wenceslaus Square—a great rectangular area in the center of Prague where thousands of angry Czechs had mobbed—and could hear a man shouting, "Shoot the traitors Chamberlain and Daladier!" followed by wild applause from those nearby. Czech policemen in dark blue uniforms were cordoning off the crowd from the main thoroughfare, which had been cleared for the tanks.

Dusk was setting in and it was beginning to snow. Suddenly, I heard someone singing the Czech national anthem. Soon the entire crowd had joined in and, like a great mournful wave, the strains of the old hymn rolled across the square in the dying light. "Where is my home? Where is my home?" It was the defiant farewell of a betrayed and conquered nation.

Even though the policemen had locked arms and formed a human chain of blue uniforms to hold back the crowd, they, too, were singing. Some were weeping openly. The Czech policemen usually seemed so tall in their resplendent uniforms with brass buttons; now I felt sorry for them. They looked like pallbearers at a funeral. Prague's last day of freedom was coming to an end.

Darkness had settled over the chanting crowd below my window now, and the familiar melody of the anthem filled me with sadness. Then I heard a different sound: the unmistakable clatter of tanks. I recognized it from the year before on the Ringstrasse of Vienna. Suddenly, out of the gloom, the first German Panzer became visible. It rounded the corner and slowly, menacingly, rattled up St. Wenceslaus Square on its way toward the parliament building. It was followed by another, and yet another, until the entire square was covered with gray-green Nazi tanks. The rumbling was so deafening it almost drowned out the singing.

The tanks had pushed the crowd back toward the parliament building, which stood as the symbol of Czechoslovakia's sovereignty. The policemen pleaded with their countrymen to give way, but to no avail. The crowd, thousands of chanting Czechs, stood fast, defiantly confronting their German conquerors. The noise of the idling Panzers mingled as a macabre counterpoint to the final stanza of the Czech national anthem bursting forth from a thousand throats.

Suddenly, a lone woman with a kerchief around her head and clutching a little flag stepped out of the crowd and slowly walked toward the lead tank. About halfway to it, she threw herself on the ground directly in its path. The crowd had stopped singing now, and then, silently, more women prostrated themselves, blocking the German advance. Within a few minutes, hundreds were lying face down in the slush of St. Wenceslaus Square, literally covering the last bit of free Czech soil with their bodies. On a signal of the lead tank, the other Panzers rolled up and confronted the desperate women in one massive row of power and steel. Then they lowered their guns. But the women did not stir.

After a minute's hesitation, the lead tank aimed its gun at one of the Czech policemen standing by. A shot rang out. I saw the tall man in the blue uniform crumple to the ground, followed by two more policemen as the tank fired two more volleys. A long and terrible silence descended over the square. Suddenly, two small children approached one of the prostrate women and tugged at her elbow. They seemed to be pleading with her to rise and, after a short struggle, the woman obeyed and accompanied her children back into the waiting crowd. Slowly, heavily, hundreds of women picked themselves up from the cold, wet cobblestones and shuffled back into the darkness, following the first woman's example. With the showdown over, the Panzers raised their guns and resumed their advance toward the parliament.

I was left shaking. Between sobs, I felt Mama's hand on my head. "Do not forget this," she said. "Never forget." Then she closed the window.

Shortly after, when Reinhard Heydrich was installed in Prague as Reichsprotektor of Bohemia and Moravia, Trudy decided to take no chances with her daughter's life. Susi was successfully placed on a list of children to be sent to safety in England on Kindertransport.

The day of our parting came in October of 1939. My mother and I went to the train station to say good-bye. Trudy became hysterical and ran screaming alongside the train as it pulled away. My mother dragged her to a bench but was unable to stop her from screaming. I looked numbly at the scene. Two years later, Trudy was deported to Auschwitz, never to return.

Mama had taken a lover named Oskar. He was a tall man who looked like a Prussian officer; indeed, he had served as a lieutenant in World War I and liked to tell a story about how, on one occasion, he had seen the German Kaiser. Now he was a Jewish refugee. He took an instant dislike to me, which I heartily reciprocated. Whenever he appeared at the apartment, he made me feel that I was in the way. He took almost all of Mama's time and, because of it, I was left alone a great deal.

One day, Mama asked me, with some embarrassment, whether I could bring myself to address her friend as Uncle Oskar. I must have gone pale because she hugged me tightly. Then she announced hesitantly, "I have decided to marry him."

"Do you love him, Mutti?" I asked as my heart pounded.

"He is in love with me," my mother answered.

"But do *you* love him?" I insisted.

For a long time, Mama did not reply. Then she said, "These are bad times for us, terrible times. I am afraid to be alone. And you need a father."

"I am afraid of him," I said without thinking. The words had come out involuntarily. Cold with fear, I held on to my mother's hand.

"And I am afraid of Hitler," she said, reaching for my other hand. Thus we sat, huddled together, for a long time. Two weeks later, Oskar and Mama married.

From that point on, my life went from bad to worse, especially in school. Once more, the classrooms were filled with uniformed

Hitler Youth, and I again was the outsider suffering their insults and beatings. Once, in the middle of a history class, there was a rough knock at the door. Six Hitlerjugend with swastika armbands and silver daggers stormed into the room, faced the class, saluted, and announced in unison: "All Jews must leave the school within the next five minutes." Our teacher, with rare presence of mind, pointed to a painting of Christ that was hanging on the wall and asked innocently, "Should he go, too?"

He got only blank stares in return.

I rose nonetheless, got my belongings together, and walked to the door. The six Nazi boys, however, armed with rubber truncheons, were blocking the exit. Screaming with delight, they dragged me to the window and pushed me out. I landed in a pile of rubble a few feet below the window, where other Hitler Youths pulled me out and beat me unconscious. Some hours later, I woke in the Jewish hospital covered with bruises. It seemed like Vienna all over again.

Life continued to get worse. I was required to wear a yellow Star of David whenever I left the house. I was not permitted to play in the park, to use a streetcar, to ride in a cab, or to leave the house after six o'clock in the evening. At home, things weren't much better. Oskar had taken to beating me regularly for the slightest infraction of his draconian house rules. Since our living quarters consisted of two small rooms, I was never more than a few feet from his glowering presence. I came to fear his brutality as much as that of the Nazis.

Mama, afraid to protect me against him, lapsed into a kind of passive melancholia and spent hours staring at the walls. I spent as little time at home as possible. Whenever I could, I fled to my grandparents' home where, as the only grandchild, I felt loved and secure. Sometimes I would weep in my grandmother's arms.

"Oskar is like Hitler," I blurted out once.

"Maybe that's why he understands him," my grandmother said cryptically, and then stared out the window in silence. I looked at her. Then she added mysteriously, "And perhaps that will save you."

On one occasion, I came home about fifteen minutes late.

"Where have you been?" Oskar shouted.

"I tried to pick some wildflowers in the forest for Mama," I answered without thinking.

Oskar grumbled something but decided not to hit me. My mother smiled at me affectionately. The truth was that I hadn't looked for flowers; I had simply forgotten the time. But to admit that fact would have meant a vicious beating, so it was easier to lie.

Gradually, lying to Oskar became second nature to me, and I learned to do anything to please Mama so that she would protect me against Oskar. Between my lies to him and my efforts to manipulate my mother, the truth became a casualty. I gradually lost sight of everything else in my overriding search for safety. Worse than that, I no longer knew quite who I was, save that I was a liar, and for that I was punished with the most effective weapons of them all: a guilty conscience and the deepening conviction that Oskar was quite right when, in his rages, he would scream that I would come to a bad end.

Every Sunday, my grandparents would drive to a nursing home in the outskirts of Prague to visit my ninety-year-old great-grandmother. Though quite frail, the old lady had retained a lucid mind and an extraordinary sense of humor. She prided herself on her agnosticism. Her closest companion in the home was an old Catholic woman of the Czech aristocracy who loved my great-grandmother but was eager to convert her.

"She told me yesterday that she will need a lady-in-waiting in heaven," great-grandmother said, wiping away tears of laughter, "and she has asked me to assist her in dressing for the resurrection."

One Sunday, however, I saw great-grandmother cry for the first time. She embraced my grandparents for a long time. The nursing home was to be closed and the patients shipped to what would later become Theresienstadt concentration camp.

"We will be with you soon," grandmother sobbed, while I tried my best to comfort her.

By late 1940, most of Europe was in Hitler's grip, and terrible fights had erupted between my stepfather and my grandparents, my mother caught in the middle. My stepfather, who, as my grandmother had observed, seemed to understand Hitler, insisted upon leaving Europe immediately.

"You are an adventurer!" my grandparents shouted. "This is after all the twentieth century. It can't get any worse."

However, evidence to the contrary was mounting steadily. The war against the Jews had begun in earnest, and by January 1941, my stepfather was dragging my mother and me to dozens of consulates in Prague, begging for visas.

Finally, an official at the Chinese Embassy, in a gesture of compassion, granted us a visa to Shanghai in exchange for "landing money," which cost us most of our belongings. The Chinese visa was useless, however, unless we could procure a transit visa to cross the Soviet Union. This was nearly impossible without being able to prove that we could leave the Soviet Union, and then somehow get to Shanghai. This meant another transit visa, this time via Japan.

But it was well known in Prague's Jewish community that the Japanese were sympathetic to the Germans and, therefore, reluctant to help the Jews. Thus, without this indispensable Japanese link in the chain of flight, the Shanghai visa was now worthless.

Mama looked more and more haggard during this time, but I cherished the moments I spent alone with her. Whenever I heard Oskar's heavy footsteps on the stairs, my heart would contract with fear. Dinners usually took place in oppressive silence with only the most obligatory conversation.

In February 1941, however, long lines suddenly formed in front of the Japanese Consulate. News had spread like wildfire that a new consul was issuing Japanese transit visas via Kobe to hundreds of desperate Jews.

After several days in line, we were ushered into the office of an elegant, kind-looking Japanese man. He leaned down to me and asked if I could speak any Japanese. I said, "Hai. Banzai," words I had learned from my schoolmates. I had no idea what they meant. He laughed, patted me on the head, and issued us three visas without the slightest difficulty. I don't recall learning his name.

"Good luck," he said to us in German as the next applicants were ushered in. Three days later, my stepfather procured the transit visa across Russia—the final link in the chain—by bribing an official of the Soviet Intourist agency.

That evening, Oskar looked at me across the table and announced coldly, "You had better pack your things. We are leaving Prague next week."

The departure date was set for March 4, 1941, my mother's birthday.

I looked at my mother, imploring her to explain.

"Oskar has been working very hard to get us visas," Mama said uncertainly, reaching for my hand.

"Must we really go?" I choked out.

Oskar glared at me and, putting both of his elbows on the table, said, "Yes, we must really go. Yes, there is no other choice. And no, your grandparents cannot come along. These three visas to cross

Russia cost a fortune. All my money. All your mother's money."
Then he added coldly, "And all your grandparents' money. So they
must stay here. And they *will* stay here."

I stared at Oskar. For two years, I had silently endured his beatings and his curses, but that was me. Now it was them, my grandparents, and that was too much. I loved my grandparents more
than anything else in the world and Oskar had now committed the
ultimate crime: he had plundered my grandparents' savings and was
separating Mama and me from them forever.

All I could do was glare at him and shriek, "What? Can't I . . ."

"Shut up, you little fool," he said angrily, cutting me off.

"It will pass!" my mother suddenly cried out. "It will pass! You
can't. We cannot . . ."

"We have to get out, and there is very little time. The handwrit-
ing is on the wall, I know it."

Oskar turned to her and froze her with a look of cold contempt.

"Listen," he said, "these are illegal visas, which are already paid for
and which could cost us our lives. They have already cost us every
cent we have. If one word of this leaks out from either of you, we
will all die in a concentration camp. Do you understand?"

His face was very close to hers now.

"And you," he said, pointing his finger across the table at me.
"You, I swear, if any word gets out, I will kill you personally. I swear
I will do it myself."

This threat finally enraged my mother. "Oskar!" she shouted at
him. "Stop!"

It was the first time I had ever heard Mama oppose Oskar. She
was crying now, calling him "an adventurer" and shrieking that
he had "bankrupted my family." At last, hands pressed to her tem-
ples, she broke down into uncontrollable sobs and rushed out of
the room.

Oskar and I sat for a long time, silent and alone. The only sounds, aside from my mother's sobs, were the ticking of the mantel clock and Oskar's labored breathing. I could see he was working himself up into a terrible rage, and God only knew what would happen. The tiny room seemed to grow even smaller, and Oskar's face became a mask of cold fury.

But when he spoke to me, it was with an eerie softness. Between clenched teeth, he said to me, "Someday you will thank me, you little bastard. Someday when the others are dead and you are alive, you will remember. You will remember that you owe me your life. God knows what you did to deserve it, but you will owe me that."

I stared at the table and said nothing.

Oskar continued, his voice still soft, yet menacing. "The others are fools. They do not understand Hitler and his kind. But I do."

At that moment, I realized I feared Oskar as much as I feared Satan. Yet, I could not resist one more plea. I whispered, "Omi and Opi cannot go?"

The question fell on deaf ears.

In the other room, Mama was wailing now. Oskar, his rage slowly subsiding, continued staring at me across the table with haunted eyes.

"Then where are we going this time?" I asked, my voice starting to crack.

He was silent for a long moment and then said matter-of-factly, "To China."

"I am not going, I am not going," I screamed, out of control. "Not without you!"

I had run all the way to my grandparents' house, and grandfather now took me by the hand and led me to the chessboard. But I was inconsolable.

"I love you, I love you," I sobbed. "I can't leave without you."

"We love you, too," said my grandfather, gently taking me in his arms, "and that's why you must go. We are old, Hitler can no longer harm us, but you must have a future."

"But why can't you go, too?" I insisted.

"We couldn't get a visa. We are too old," grandfather replied softly. His kind eyes glistened with tears behind the pince-nez spectacles he wore. "You must be strong and brave now," he said. "You are thirteen, almost a man."

I looked at him gratefully. "And where is China?" I asked.

The old man put his arm around my shoulder and led me to a map that was hanging on the wall in his study. Slowly, he traced the route to China with his finger. "It is on the other side of the world," he said with a sigh.

The day of our departure was drawing near. The journey to China was to take us across Siberia and Japan, with our final destination being Shanghai, China's largest city. Mama had told me it was the only place in the entire world to which Oskar had been able to get us an entrance visa. Oskar and Mama were busy packing. I was told to pack a small suitcase. Only essentials could go, Oskar explained, and nothing of value could be taken across the German border. I prayed that something would happen to wake me from what I believed to be a nightmare. But the nightmare was reality.

Finally, the morning of my Mama's birthday arrived. We were to board a train for Moscow that night. Grandmother prepared dinner but only Oskar ate. During the meal, when Oskar wasn't looking, grandmother handed Mama her most prized possession: a large diamond brooch framed in an antique platinum setting, which my mother quickly slipped into her purse. At dusk, Oskar hailed a taxi and asked the driver to take us to the station. Since Mama and Oskar spoke German, no questions were asked. My grandparents were to follow in another taxi, to bid us farewell.

As we drove through Prague for that last time, it occurred to me that we were violating at least three anti-Jewish laws: we were out after six, weren't wearing our yellow stars, and were traveling by taxi. I desperately hoped that we would be stopped and forced to return home, but we reached the station without incident. Passengers were already boarding the Moscow train, and a conductor took us to our assigned compartment. I immediately lowered the window and looked up and down the platform, hoping to find my grandparents. They were nowhere to be seen.

The train was scheduled to leave at eight o'clock. The large station clock showed seven forty-five. My mother was desperate with anguish. I, too, was frantic. Neither one of us had said good-bye to my grandparents. Oskar sat impassively. My eyes darted from the platform to the minute hand on the station clock. At five minutes to eight, I finally saw my grandparents.

"Here we are!" I shouted. They heard me and came running to the train window. Although I knew it was against the rules, I no longer cared—I turned around, dashed to the exit, and jumped off the train into my grandmother's arms. Oskar's face appeared at the open window, contorted with rage.

"I am not going with you," I screamed at the top of my lungs. "You are not my father. I am staying here."

Two SS officers, startled by the commotion, looked at me with idle curiosity.

"Then go and kill yourself, you bastard, like your father did," Oskar yelled.

It was two minutes past eight. The train sputtered and creaked alive. With all his strength, my grandfather picked me up and put me on the step as the train began to move. As Mama pulled me in, I looked back into the night—grandfather's flashlight was moving in the distance, up and down, up and down. Then it was gone.

The train chugged through the night. I peered out the window at the snowy landscape rushing by, noting how serene and tranquil it all was in the light of the moon. Oskar was snoring and Mama, after having taken a sedative, had fallen into a fitful slumber. I wanted to ask her whether what Oskar had said about Papa was true, but I was afraid to wake her. The grief of leaving my grandparents kept me from sleeping, so I counted the little Czech villages as the train steamed toward Poland. Then I remembered what the geography teacher had told us: there was no more Poland, and the German Reich now shared a common border with the Soviet Union.

Toward morning, the door of our compartment opened. I was almost dozing and did not see the man who had entered. My first view of him was at floor level, which was enough to make me panic, for what I saw was a pair of black military boots. Then I heard two words that made my heart race with terror: "Heil Hitler!"

When I looked up, I first saw Oskar. Incredibly, he had jumped up and was saluting, returning the entering man's "Heil" with the precision and authority of a well-trained German officer.

Then I looked at the man, whom Oskar had saluted, standing in the compartment door and in a Wehrmacht uniform. Not just any uniform, but the awesome, be-ribboned dress tunic of a high-ranking Nazi officer. I realized that a Wehrmacht colonel was about to join us in our journey to the Soviet Union.

Shaken by fear and nausea, I wondered whether Oskar's reaction was a reflex from his war years, or whether it was an act, a demonstration of his instinct for survival. Either way, the scene was ghastly: Oskar frozen in a stiff salute, Hitler's name spoken proudly still lingering on his lips. It seemed that, alongside the Wehrmacht colonel, Oskar was now in his true element.

Almost immediately, Oskar produced a bottle of rare cognac—given to us by Omi and Opi—and offered a toast to the Fuehrer, followed by another, and yet another. It all seemed like a hideous joke: three homeless Jews fleeing from the Holocaust, and here was my stepfather toasting the Third Reich with a Wehrmacht officer. I sat there paralyzed and listened to their war stories and watched them drink and toast—they even sang. I thought of Omi and Opi, now abandoned to the Nazis. Oskar might as well have toasted the devil.

And yet, this man I hated with a black bottomless hate was saving my life and the life of my helpless mother. So visible was our grief that the colonel's suspicions would almost certainly have been aroused. But Oskar's "Sieg Heils" were so utterly convincing that the colonel soon regarded us as friends and allies. He leaned toward Oskar and whispered with a conspiratorial smile, "When the time comes, we shall squeeze the life out of those Bolshevik dogs. Our Fuehrer knows exactly what to do." His large hands were choking an imaginary Bolshevik. Exhausted, he leaned back in his corner. "I wonder when they will serve us breakfast on this train," he then muttered to no one in particular.

Oskar drew forth a paper bag and offered it to the colonel. I noticed that it contained our last Prague supper—several pieces of fried chicken and some potato salad—carefully wrapped in wax paper. Oskar and his Nazi friend hungrily consumed every last morsel.

I fell into a terrible despair as I watched the two men eat. I began to cry quietly, and when the colonel asked me what was wrong, I could only sob, "Omi and Opi," and then, "Papa, Papa."

I knew immediately that I had made a terrible mistake by losing control over my feelings and that Oskar was now livid with rage. So I suppressed my tears and kept quiet as Oskar glared at me.

Eventually the colonel fell asleep and began to snore. Oskar got up from his seat and walked over to my corner.

"Come with me," he commanded in a voice that brooked no opposition. Numb with fear, I obeyed. Oskar's drinking with the Wehrmacht colonel had terrified me.

I followed him silently out of the compartment and down the corridor. He opened the door of the men's toilet and ordered me to enter. After looking over his shoulder, he followed me in, quickly pulling the door shut behind him. Then he turned toward me, eyes blazing with a murderous fury. The blows that followed came quickly and hard. Soon my nose was bleeding and I was sobbing with terror, but my screams were drowned out by the noise of the train.

"Listen, you bastard, and listen well," Oskar threatened. "I have told them you are my son, because your mother didn't want to leave you behind. Your father is dead. If you mention his name, I will kill you with my bare hands." I was terrified. "Do you have anything that bears your father's name?"

Trembling, I pulled out a faded photograph of Papa I had carried around in my pocket for years.

"Hand it to me," Oskar commanded. He looked at the photograph, turned it over and saw where my mother had written in ink, "Karl Hirschfeld."

"Karl!" he said with a sneer. He tore the little memento in half and flushed it down the toilet. At that very moment, I was no longer a child.

"Anything else?" he barked.

I remained silent, which only elicited another blow from him.

"Anything else?" he repeated.

I shook my head. All I had left of Papa was now gone. I looked at Oskar. I hated him, but also realized that I owed him my life. Perhaps he was right: I would have to give up Papa, and now it was a matter of choosing between Oskar and Hitler. Everything within me went cold. I was on my own.

We returned to the compartment. The colonel had awakened by now, and he greeted Oskar like a long-lost friend. The train was beginning to slow down and Mama, seeming nervous, kept fidgeting with her purse. Suddenly, she opened it and took out the diamond brooch grandmother had given to her before we left. After a moment's hesitation, she lowered the compartment window and threw the shiny object out into the dawn. No one had noticed anything. My mother sat down heavily, her face buried in her hands.

Shortly afterward, a Nazi border official entered. "Passports, please!" he announced.

The colonel grunted something and handed the man a piece of paper with a large swastika embossed on it in gold. The official sprang to attention and saluted stiffly. Then Oskar handed him a document.

"Your son?" the official said, waving in my direction.

Oskar nodded.

"Open the luggage," the Nazi commanded, raking Oskar with a hard, suspicious stare. Oskar nervously reached for the nearest suitcase; he was aware that all families leaving Germany were viewed with suspicion.

"*Heraus!*" the Wehrmacht colonel screamed suddenly in a military tone. "They are my friends."

"Jawohl, Herr Obersturmbannfuehrer!" The border guard clicked his heels and fled from the compartment with an obsequious bow. Soon afterward, the train rolled into the border station.

The colonel, whom Oskar had courted so successfully, got off after kissing Mama's hand.

I looked out the window. The small station seemed to be divided into two separate parts. On the left, there was a picture of Hitler, draped with a swastika. On the right fluttered a crimson banner with the portrait of a kind-looking elderly man with a mustache.

"Who is that?" I asked.

"Stalin," replied Oskar. "And don't ask any more questions."

A Soviet customs official came in and glanced at our bags.

"Is that all?" he asked.

Oskar nodded again. The man stamped the suitcases and left.

Suddenly, Mama began to cry hysterically. She was still sobbing when the train began to move. Stalin's picture floated by, smiling benignly.

"At last, a free country," Oskar said.

Chapter 3

Shanghai, 1941–1947

The Trans-Siberian Express was a comfortable train. We had boarded it in Moscow and now, after ten days of travel punctuated by occasional brief stops, we had crossed the Urals and were traversing Siberia. I sat near the window and gazed at the landscape. Gradually, forests gave way to the snow-covered tundra. The high northern latitude, the extreme slants of the rays of the wintry sun, the flatness of the terrain—all these combined to create everywhere a sense of immense space, distance, and power. The heaven was vast, the skyline remote and extended. I felt the proximity of the great wilderness of the Russian North—silent, somber, infinitely patient. The white moonlit nights had an unbelievable eerie poetry, their loneliness resonating with mine.

Once a day, while the train was taking on coal, we were allowed to get off and exercise by walking briskly up and down the station platform of some remote Siberian town. The temperature was always arctic.

"Don't pee in the snow," warned the friendly old conductor who seemed to be a relic from the days of the czar, "or your little thing will turn into an icicle."

Old grandmothers with weather-beaten faces tried to sell us goat's milk and hard-boiled eggs. In Irkutsk, a whole detachment of soldiers got on the train. They were good natured and one of them played the harmonica for me. To the intense displeasure of the meticulous Oskar, a Red Army officer kept urinating into the washbasin. He did so from a measured distance, with amazing precision, and with consummate artistry. Oskar glared at him, but said nothing. The officer grinned back broadly.

The journey through Siberia seemed endless. Most of the time, I stared out at the vast expanses of the Russian landscape, almost eerie in its snow-covered silence. We shared a compartment with a Japanese diplomat who introduced himself as Dr. Ryoichi Manabe. He was being transferred from Berlin to Shanghai to a new diplomatic post, he explained to us in fluent German. He seemed quite young, perhaps in his early thirties, and had a courtly, gentle manner about him.

We shared our meals with him, and I played chess with him occasionally. After the first week of the long journey, my mother mentioned to him that we, too, were headed for Shanghai, as refugees. After all, the Japanese consul in Prague had helped us and she saw no reason to fear this nice young man, so well versed in German literature.

Four weeks after we had left Moscow, the train pulled into Vladivostok harbor.

"Over there is Alaska and America," Dr. Manabe said, pointing across the Bering Sea. "Is that where you will be going?"

"No," I replied, wishing I could answer yes. "We are heading for China."

Before we parted, he handed us his card and invited my mother, quite matter-of-factly, to call him in Shanghai, if we should ever need his help.

From Vladivostok, a small boat took us to the Japanese port of Kobe, from where it would be another month before a Chinese cargo ship could carry us to Shanghai. When we finally disembarked, among a horde of coolies, rickshaws, and dockworkers, it was June 1941. The heat was stifling as I looked around in bewilderment. A newspaper headline at a nearby stand caught my eye. GERMANY INVADES RUSSIA, it said. I was frightened. Hitler seemed to be following us halfway around the world.

One hundred years before we had landed in Shanghai, the colorful Chinese port had been divided among several Western nations. Each of these foreign countries had carved out a part of the city for itself that each regarded virtually as its property, as opposed to that of the Chinese. Thus, one section resembled an English provincial town and prided itself on a main street named after Queen Victoria, as well as for a British public school for boys in which I was enrolled. Adjacent to it, there was a French "concession" in which Oskar and Mama rented a modest apartment and where Oskar found a job as a teller in an import-export bank while my mother developed a talent for making hats for elderly ladies. On the other side of the city, there was the German settlement with a high school named after Kaiser Wilhelm.

Soon after we arrived, my mother insisted Oskar adopt me to lessen the chance of bureaucratic problems in the future. Oskar agreed for clerical practicality, not for love. My mother told me I needed a father and she thought giving me his name would make that true. Nothing could have been further from the truth. I had already lost my little photograph of my real father and now I was about to lose his name as well. I never felt more alone than I did that day. My schoolmates in Vienna were gone. My grandparents were gone. My father was gone. I was on my own.

The Chinese were generally reduced to second-class status in these foreign sections and forced to live in the slums. Chinese law did not apply in any of the "extraterritorial settlements." Instead, the English teachers at the public school taught us Rudyard Kipling's *White Man's Burden*. I was told that I would have to study English, French, and Chinese. Fortunately, I had a musical ear and languages came easily to me. Life was bearable again. Oskar had even stopped beating me.

One day in December, this colonial splendor came to a sudden end. The Japanese had attacked the United States at Pearl Harbor, and Shanghai came under Japanese martial law. The German community prevailed on its Japanese allies to round up all the Jews and force them to move into a ghetto surrounded by barbed wire and guarded by Japanese sentries with fierce police dogs. Swastikas became visible all over the German settlement and the Kaiser Wilhelm School was renamed for Adolf Hitler.

Mama began to cry again. One day she became hysterical. A letter had arrived from my grandparents. It had been mailed from Theresienstadt and had taken six months to reach China. They wrote that they had been deported from Prague four weeks after our departure. Mama feared for their lives.

Oskar's situation at work was tenuous and he had taken to beating me again. I almost felt sorry for him. He had saved us from Hitler and had brought us halfway across the world. Yet here we were, still in Hitler's power, facing the prospect of a Jewish ghetto in China.

I recall my mother agonizing over whether she should take up Dr. Manabe's invitation to call him. After all, the political situation had deteriorated drastically since that long trek across Siberia. However, we knew nothing about Dr. Manabe except that he was assigned to Shanghai as part of the Japanese Diplomatic Corps. Finally, with the move to the ghetto only three days away, my mother decided to take the chance and see him. Since my stepfather had developed a heart ailment and was afraid to accompany her, he and I spent the day anxiously awaiting her return. She came back later that evening, her eyes shining.

Dr. Manabe had been as kind as ever. Not only had he remembered us, but when my mother asked him to allow us to remain outside the ghetto, he immediately issued a one-year extension of stay so that my stepfather could be near a good hospital. I could continue my education at the British public school, where the teachers protested against the Japanese occupation of the city by continuing to teach us Shakespeare. My mother had proved to be a brave woman. We were all relieved.

The school I attended offered a strange mixture of excellence and brutality. The British and French teachers, stranded in Shanghai and unable to go home, were soon replaced by others of "neutral" nationalities. I immersed myself in *Hamlet* and acted the part of the Danish prince in a school play, imagining that King Claudius was Oskar and giving a creditable performance. The hatreds of the war were reflected among the pupils. Racial tensions were rampant and beatings were common. On one occasion, a number of boys had torn off my shirt and were taking turns hitting me with a bamboo cane. The biggest of the bullies offered the cane to a Russian boy standing nearby and ordered him to join in the beating.

"Hit him, or you will get the same medicine," he was told.

The skinny Russian boy took the piece of bamboo, broke it in half, and crossed his arms. From that moment on, the frail lad, named Rusty, and I became inseparable.

Rusty was a quiet, fair-haired boy with a gift for drawing and painting. Like me, he was somewhat of a loner. But unlike me, he was deeply religious. Rusty could talk for hours about the nature of God.

"Before you are born," he said one night, "God sorts out your soul. If you've got a round soul, he puts you on a round planet; if you've got an oval soul, he puts you on an oval planet."

"So what's your soul like?" I wanted to know.

"In my case, God made a mistake," Rusty said sadly. "I've got an oval soul, and he put me on a round planet. And the school keeps trying to file my soul round like everyone else's."

Rusty's favorite writer was the French aviator Antoine de Saint-Exupéry, whose *Little Prince* was published in the middle of the war that was now so forcefully altering my life. Rusty was fascinated by the sad little boy who was the ruler and sole inhabitant of asteroid B-612. When we learned in 1944 that the flier had not returned from a mission over his Nazi-occupied homeland, Rusty was inconsolable. "He's gone to look for the little prince," he said.

Rusty's mother was a fortune-teller who lived in a two-room flat near the ghetto. She said she had been married to a Russian count who had been killed during the Bolshevik revolution. Rusty's own origins were a mystery. We would sit with her in the afternoons before she went to work, and she would pour us endless cups of tea from a large potbellied samovar. Then she would examine my palms and tell my future. It was always the same: I would go to America after the war and make my fortune.

Rusty assured me that his mother was a palmist of excellent reputation. She had predicted a fine future for him in Australia. We trusted her implicitly but begged her to tell us if there was a way for us to stay together.

"No," she said mockingly, "and you should be grateful that I don't predict your death by an American bomb."

At least once a week, Shanghai was subjected to aerial bombardment. The American B-29s targeted the Japanese military installations on the outskirts of the city, but they frequently missed and hit our area instead. There were few air-raid shelters since the city was built on swampland, and so Rusty and I would often simply look up at the attacking planes and wish that we could fly back with them to America.

Oskar and my mother were more miserable now than ever as the raids increased in ferocity. My mother found the courage to ask Dr. Manabe for extensions twice more, and both times he complied. Nevertheless, I spent less and less time at home because of their discomfort. Instead, Rusty and I would sometimes sit in his little room and talk about God. I had become confused by the fact that each army in the war appealed for victory to the same God. I imagined that perhaps God was an old general with a vast closet full of different uniforms, spending all his time changing from one into another and then rushing off to lead an army. I felt sorry for him and for what seemed to be his thankless job.

As Rusty was so attracted to spiritualism, one night during a particularly violent raid, we tried to conjure up the spirits of our dead fathers. Nothing happened. Rusty explained this by saying that he had no likeness of his father and therefore was unable to conjure his image. I tried to conjure Papa's face from the memory of the faded photograph Oskar had flushed down the toilet, to no avail. Papa did not appear, either. Instead, the all clear sounded and we crept up on the roof of a nearby whorehouse to shoot down Japanese planes. The objective was to get an erection as quickly as possible while lying on our backs. Aiming our "weapons" at the gray dawn above the city, we imagined dozens of planes falling out of the sky. By morning, our depression had vanished.

Rusty and I were the only virgins left in our class and, being sixteen, were entirely consumed with sexual urgency. I was writing poetry by then and was told by the teacher that I had considerable talent. Some of my classmates felt that my poetry would improve even further if I could draw on some real experience for my love poems. An Indian student who prided himself on his sexual exploits took up a collection for me among my classmates, the ultimate goal being the financing of a visit to the neighborhood brothel.

I was reluctant, but acquiesced after consulting with Rusty. He even advised that an hour of conversation should be included in the price, so that I could better benefit from the experience as a poet.

The bordellos of Shanghai, like the schools, mirrored the racial divisions of the war. Chinese girls were readily available and fetched the lowest fees, largely catering to the enlisted men of the Japanese occupational army. Some of the more exclusive downtown brothels, which serviced German businessmen and Japanese army high officers, supplied white women of uncertain age and ancestry. These ladies prided themselves on their French or Russian accents and alleged links to European nobility. Chinese money had become almost worthless. Rates changed daily, often hourly, and always up. It was not unusual to carry around a suitcase full of paper currency. Sometimes the prices changed while one waited in line to pay. Barter was also common. Negotiations for bordello services were no exception.

On the appointed day, I marched down to the bordello, accompanied by ten financial contributors, all of whom were eager to witness the results of my practical education. Sarkari, the Indian entrepreneur, had chosen the Golden Dragon for me. She was a good-natured Chinese prostitute who weighed more than three hundred pounds, and prided herself on a row of golden teeth and an enormous posterior. On slow evenings, she would bet a client on whether she could pull a nail out of the wall with her buttocks. It was said that considerable sums had changed hands on such nights, and that it was prudent to wager on the side of "the

Dragon." Sarkari assured me that an hour's conversation had been negotiated: half an hour before and half an hour after. Rusty slipped me a nail file. "In case she becomes dangerous," he said, offering what he could to protect me.

When we arrived at the house, business seemed brisk and none of the whores were visible on the veranda. Sarkari rang the bell and Ma, the corpulent madam, appeared at the door. He flashed his most seductive smile but Ma waved him away with a peremptory gesture. It seemed that something had gone wrong. After another appeal, Sarkari walked over to me and announced glumly, "Prices have gone up again because of inflation. You can have sex with her, but you can't talk to her. There is no time for the scheduled conversation." After a hurried consultation, we gave in—things had gone too far, and there was no turning back.

Trying to hide my nervousness, I followed the Golden Dragon up the stairs while the contributors waited below. I had dressed for the occasion—in my only good suit—and was perspiring profusely. The Dragon, smiling her golden smile, walked over to me and loosened my tie. She slipped out of her dress and enormous rolls of fat cascaded down over her hips. Stark naked, she began to take off my shirt. Frantic with fear, I pointed toward three whips hanging on the wall. They reminded me of those in the headmaster's office at school and seemed to be the only possible topic of conversation—I was desperate to avert a complete fiasco although I knew that my initiation, with or without conversation, was in serious jeopardy. The Dragon, noticing my diversionary maneuver, took one of the whips off the wall and lashed me gently across the flanks. *She is becoming dangerous,* I thought, remembering Rusty's nail file. I pulled out the little weapon and pointed it at the Dragon. The woman looked at my hand and stopped smiling. Instead of stopping her whipping, she hit me harder and pushed me toward the door with a violent curse.

"Out," she screamed at the top of her lungs. "Out, you crazy little bastard!"

I stumbled down the stairs while the Dragon, still cursing, threw my shirt and tie down after me. Then she slammed the door.

"What the hell happened?" asked Sarkari. I must have looked like death, as his voice betrayed genuine concern.

"You idiot," Sarkari continued with a laugh, "she probably thought you were a masochist and wanted to do you a favor."

I didn't know what he was talking about. "Don't tell the others," I begged.

The shame almost choked me. Rusty came up and put his arm around me. I gave him back his nail file and told him everything. When I had finished, Rusty looked thoughtful.

"The same thing would have happened to me," he said. "I think you and I must be in love before we can do it. And it's not going to happen to us here."

I looked at him gratefully. We walked away together and began to talk about America.

In the spring of 1945, my mother suffered a nervous breakdown and had to enter a hospital. She had learned that, sometime during the year of 1942, my grandparents had been transported to Treblinka and they had perished there in the gas chambers. I tried to comfort her, but she was inconsolable. The guilt of having left her parents behind consumed her. Oskar, for his own part, was now alone in the little one-room flat. I had moved in with Rusty. Rusty and I had a few silkworms on the windowsill and the only food they ate was the leaf of the mulberry tree, which they ate ravenously. On occasion, his mother needed our room for a special customer. At such times, we roamed the outskirts of the city, hunting for mulberry leaves.

After a few weeks, our worms shed their iridescent skins so they could continue to grow. Then they would spin a white or pink cocoon of pure silk and, within a month, a moth would emerge. The moths would live for only a week. Eating nothing, all they did was copulate.

Fascinated, we paired them off and watched them glued together in the act of reproduction. Shortly afterward, the female moths would swell up and lay hundreds of little yellow eggs the size of pinheads. Then the moths died, but as soon as the weather became warm again, the eggs would pop and tiny worms would wriggle out.

Now it was May and a few of the worms had just begun to work on their cocoons. One day, Rusty rushed in, breathlessly waving a newspaper.

"Hitler is dead!" he shouted.

We did not sleep that night; we knew now that the war could not last too much longer.

Yet the summer of 1945 was terrible. Order was breaking down in Shanghai, which was the last remaining major city under Japanese military occupation. Food was scarce and the American bombers paid us nightly visits, making sleep impossible. School was eventually suspended, and Rusty and I began roaming the streets instead, looking for food.

In August, rumors swept through the city that the Americans had dropped a horrible new bomb on Japan. Mass hysteria broke out. Rape, pillage, and murder became commonplace, followed by a typhus epidemic. One day, I developed a raging fever and Rusty brought me to the local hospital.

The doctor diagnosed typhus and for several days I hovered between life and death. The hospital was under quarantine and packed with typhus patients. The beds were so close together, there was hardly any room to walk between them. On the bed to my right lay an elderly man, his cheeks hollowed out by fever and star-vation. He was so weak, he was unable to move.

"Play with yourself," he whispered to me. "So long as you can get it up, you won't die."

The next day he was dead and an orderly carried off his body. I concentrated on the face of a girl whom I would love but whom I had never seen and followed the dead man's instructions. Two weeks later, the fever had subsided and I was released from the hospital.

When the war was finally over, Rusty and I went to the highway and watched the Japanese occupation forces pull out. Two weeks later, Chinese soldiers of Chiang Kai-shek's army marched into the city. They looked starved and exhausted and wore torn boots caked with mud. The soldiers descended on the city like locusts foraging for food. It was rumored that, a few hundred miles away, a Chinese Communist army was getting ready to advance. Its leader was a man named Mao Tse-tung.

American uniforms also appeared in town. Like many of my schoolmates, I now became a shoeshine boy. One day, an American lieutenant, after praising my shine, asked me whether I wished to go to America to get a college education. "I am from a state called Iowa," he said. I had never heard of Iowa. "I went to Grinnell," he added, "you know, Gary Cooper went there." I had heard of Gary Cooper—a movie featuring him had been shown all over Shanghai and he had become my instant role model.

I began to tremble. "How can I get to a college where Gary Cooper went?"

The lieutenant smiled. "I'll write a letter for you," he offered. "Here is their address. Write them for application forms; maybe you'll get lucky."

A few weeks later, I'd let the idea of going to school in America slip to the back of my mind and had landed a job as a dockworker unloading relief supplies. From there, I managed to get a job as an interpreter in the Shanghai office of the newly established United Nations Relief and Rehabilitation Administration. My heart swelled with pride—I had heard of the creation of the United Nations at San Francisco.

I asked my new UN boss whether he could use another boy. He nodded and I ran to Rusty's house. Now we were able to work side by side, earning weekly wages, eating well, and determined as ever to make Rusty's mother's American prophecy come true.

I tried my best, through UNRRA, to trace the fate of my grandparents. I clung to the hope that, perhaps, by some miracle, they might have escaped the gas ovens of Treblinka after all. I found out their bodies had been thrown, together with those of several thousand other elderly Jews, into enormous pits that were to become their graves. In horror, I wondered what their last moments might have been. Did they speak? Did they pray? Did they cling to one another before they died? Two good people who had loved me and who had never harmed anyone; lifeless, they fell on top of corpses and other corpses fell on top of them. They are still falling.

After my mother's nervous breakdown, she and Oskar resumed living together, but I visited them only rarely. Oskar had no job, and I gave them a part of my wages every week. My mother and I had become estranged. I could not forgive her for having married Oskar, and Oskar could not forgive me for existing. Several times I asked my mother whether it was true that Papa had killed himself. Once she nodded, but when I pressed her for details, she looked away and refused to answer. Oskar stared at me with undisguised hatred. But despite his jealousy, he no longer beat me. He had become afraid.

One day, a jovial American dropped into our UNRRA office. He was introduced to me as Charles Jordan of the Jewish Joint

Distribution Committee. Mr. Jordan was a kind man interested in how young people fared and the education we had received in these difficult times. He seemed impressed that I was able to recite part of *Hamlet* by heart. To this day, I can remember every word of the famous soliloquy.

"Would you be interested in a scholarship to an American college?" he asked.

Would I be interested? I would have signed a pact with the devil!

Mr. Jordan looked at me kindly and asked me to show him my school reports, which were excellent. The headmaster had certified that I had received only two canings for misconduct and I had excelled in my English language courses and showed promise in French and Chinese. Mr. Jordan was impressed and promised that he would try his best for me. For three months, I waited in a fever of anticipation, and then, in late 1946, Mr. Jordan walked in and announced that I had been admitted to a small college in the American Midwest—with a full scholarship.

"It's called Grinnell," he said, "and it's in a state called Iowa. A very famous American actor named Gary Cooper went there." I smiled knowingly and thought I would burst with joy.

I hugged Mr. Jordan in gratitude. He revealed that he and the lieutenant I'd met as a shoe-shine boy had collaborated to make my dream come true, with the lieutenant securing my admission to Grinnell and Mr. Jordan procuring the scholarship.

Getting the documents together was no easy task, however. Countless papers were required, and the fact that I was stateless and without passport made everything more difficult. The International Refugee Organization gave me a piece of paper that certified my existence. Then I laid siege to the American Consulate, where I was informed that if I wished to go to the United States as a regular immigrant, I would have to wait until year 2050. The Austrian quota was heavily oversubscribed. But, the consul added, it was possible to go to America as a student. He would agree to give me a student visa, but I would have to sign that I would return to my place of birth or most recent residence after the expiration of my studies. I signed the document without hesitation—I would have signed anything. Then I got myself passage as a deckhand on a converted troop transporter, the USS *General Gordon*, which was to set sail for San Francisco in August of 1947. I had decided not to tell my mother about my good fortune because I was afraid she would tell Oskar and he would sabotage my plans.

Rusty, of course, knew everything. He had secured passage to Australia in exchange for pledging to work there as a laborer for two years. We reported our respective progress to Rusty's mother. Our admiration for her clairvoyant gifts had become unbounded; however, she told us to keep working. "Lady Fortune is kind to those," she liked to say, "who do not rely on her too much."

Forty-eight hours before the *General Gordon* was scheduled to leave, I still did not quite know how to break the news to Mama and Oskar. All my travel documents were in order, and I had already quit my job. I had to pack my few belongings and could no longer hide my plans.

I climbed up the stairs to the little flat for the last time and announced calmly, "I am going to America tomorrow."

Mama seemed stunned. "But what about me?" she asked fearfully.

"Mutti," I said, "I have the chance to get an education at an American college."

My mother smiled and her eyes lit up with joy. I had not seen her smile like that in years.

"God bless you, my prince," she said tenderly. "You will find your happiness and fortune in America."

"Why didn't you tell us earlier?" Oskar asked. His voice trembled with a hidden fury. I did not answer. Oskar jumped to his feet. "You are a liar and a criminal," he shrieked, lunging at me. I stepped aside. "You will end in the gutter, like your father. The curse is in your blood and even America cannot wash it clean. Go to hell!"

For the first time, I felt indifference toward this man. I had defeated him. I had won. I was on my way to freedom and he was staying behind. My only regret was for my best friend, Rusty.

Rusty had come to the dock to bid me farewell—he was to embark for Australia within a month. We had sustained each other through the war years and given each other the love we needed to stay alive. Now, we were unable to speak. It was six in the morning and the ship was scheduled to depart at seven. American soldiers were kissing their girls before boarding.

"Your mother was right," I managed to say through my tears. Then Rusty handed me a parting gift: a wooden sign with my name on it, neatly emblazoned in his artistic hand.

"My mother predicts that you will be working for the United Nations someday," Rusty said. "I made you a desk sign so that you will remember me." We embraced a long time. I gave Rusty my stamp collection, the only thing of value that I owned. We promised to write; then I went on board. Soon afterward, a siren sounded and the ship moved downriver. Standing on the dock, Rusty looked alone and forlorn. I felt guilty that I couldn't take him with me. I waved to him, and he waved back with a blue handkerchief. Then I could no longer see him. The tall buildings of the Shanghai waterfront appeared in stark silhouette against the light of early morning. I cried with happiness and pain as the sun broke through the clouds and the ship moved out into the open sea. I had entered Shanghai as Hans Hirschfeld. I was leaving as John Stoessinger.

I was on my way to a new life with a new name.

CHAPTER 4

Arrival in America, 1947

I enjoyed my duties as an auxiliary seaman on the USS *General Gordon*. In the mornings, I scrubbed down the promenade deck, put up chairs for the first-class passengers, and served refreshments from the ship's bar. In the afternoons, I helped to peel potatoes in the kitchen and set the tables in the dining room. During the second half of the two-week voyage, I was promoted to waiter and earned tips from the dinner guests. In the evening, I mingled with American soldiers who were returning home from the war. I listened to their stories but was reluctant to ask questions; I was ashamed of betraying my ignorance about their homeland. The America I knew was a land of fantasy and dreams where I was seeking refuge from a horrible reality. Slowly, I began to understand that this wonderland, too, had geography with teeming cities called New York, San Francisco, and Chicago, and that Americans were not Olympian gods but mortal men and women with a normal range of human emotions. I was astounded at their capacity for drinking liquor and by the size of the tips I pocketed. Some of the curses I heard during a midnight barroom brawl added a new dimension to my already quite extensive storehouse of profanity.

At nighttime, when I was unable to sleep, I would leave the crowded steerage quarters and climb up on the lower deck and gaze out at the gently rolling sea. During the last days of the voyage, some of the soldiers taught me games of craps and poker. On the night before our arrival in San Francisco, several poker games were in progress. Once again unable to sleep, I wandered from one makeshift table to another, watching intently.

"Want me to deal you in, kid?" one of the soldiers asked. He was flipping cards around a wooden box to six or seven other players.

"Sure," I said without hesitation. Suddenly, my entire body came alive with a powerful thrill I had never felt before; it was as though someone had turned on an electric switch inside me. Seeing that each player had a stack of chips in front of him, I pulled out a hundred dollars and handed it to the soldier with the biggest pile. It was all the money I had made in tips during the last two weeks.

The soldier looked up briefly and flicked twenty chips in my direction. I was in the game.

During the next two hours, the cards I was dealt were miserable. Too afraid to bluff, I folded one hand after another. My pile of chips was dwindling. Finally, at about four o'clock in the morning, an older soldier with a huge beard dealt me an ace. I pushed two chips toward the center of the table and received a second ace. Two more chips went into the pot. The third card was a ten, and the fourth another ten. Only three of us were left in the game: the cook, the soldier with the beard, and me. Glancing at the pot, I noted it contained well over three hundred dollars. The beard dealt the last card facedown. A third ten! I had a full house. The cook folded his hand with a curse.

"Your bet," said the beard, looking at me. I hesitated. Beads of sweat had formed on my forehead and the palms of my hands felt clammy as I pushed two more chips away from me.

The beard had watched me carefully. Suddenly, he said calmly, "Raise you a hundred," and threw ten large chips into the pot. I looked at him in consternation, but his face behind the beard betrayed no emotion. He had raised me the limit. It would cost me a hundred dollars to stay in the game. My entire fortune consisted of one hundred and twenty dollars. I trembled. If I called the hand and lost, I would arrive in San Francisco virtually penniless. If I folded, all I would lose were my earnings. I could not take the chance.

"You win," I said, and the beard raked in the pot.

"What did you have?" he asked.

"A full house."

He looked at me with disbelief. "In this game you need balls, kid," he said, turning over his five cards. All I saw was a pair of queens. He had bluffed me out. I was sick about losing my money, but I still enjoyed the excitement and the risk. I remember my mother telling me that my father liked to gamble too much. Did I inherit this interest or did I deep down want to be more like my father?

Daylight was breaking and I needed to feel the sea mist on my face. I went up to the deck, held on to the railing, and closed my eyes.

"There she is," said the beard, who had followed me up. He pointed into the distance.

Against the dawn, barely visible, was the outline of a graceful arc. "There she is, the Golden Gate," the beard repeated. "We are home."

Two hours later, we steamed into San Francisco Bay. As we passed the Golden Gate Bridge, the beard put his arm on my shoulder and said, "Throw a penny into the sea; it will bring you luck." I threw a penny over the ship's railing. Suddenly, I thought of Rusty, who would soon be embarking for Australia.

"Jesus," said the beard suddenly. I looked up. We could see a huge WELCOME HOME sign in the harbor. The soldiers were cheering, while a large crowd had gathered on the dock with women waving handkerchiefs. I thought of Rusty's lonesome figure and his blue handkerchief receding into the distance on the docks of Shanghai. It seemed like years ago. The USS *General Gordon* docked, and we disembarked. When I stepped off the ship, I fell to the ground.

"Are you okay?" asked my bearded friend. He was smoking the longest cigar I had ever seen.

"I am fine," I answered, rising quickly. I did not want him to know that I had fallen to the ground on purpose to kiss the American soil.

CHAPTER 5

Iowa, 1950

Grinnell College was a small school in the heartland of the United States. I arrived there on a beautiful autumn evening in late September and was welcomed by a kind elderly lady who introduced herself as the housemother of the dormitory that was to be my home. She had just been comforting a boy from a neighboring town who had an attack of homesickness.

"Where are you from?" she asked, turning to me.

"Shanghai," I said.

"Shanghai, what?" Mrs. Hall wanted to know.

"China," I blurted out.

Mrs. Hall looked at me in disbelief for a moment, but said nothing. Then she opened the door to a small room with a window that overlooked a row of elm trees.

"We are a small college," she said, "but we pride ourselves on our high standards." I listened respectfully as Mrs. Hall opened the window of my room to let in the evening breeze. "We do not allow any drinking, there must be absolute quiet in the house after ten o'clock, and girls must be in their dormitories by eleven."

"What girls?" I asked. Ma's bordello in Shanghai had flashed through my mind.

"We have about five hundred girls on campus," Mrs. Hall explained. "Once a month there are chaperoned dances. On those occasions, you may keep your date out until midnight; after that, she is punished and turns into a pumpkin." Mrs. Hall laughed innocently.

I stared at her in confusion; I had not yet heard the story of Cinderella.

"If you are homesick, please feel free to talk to me," she said gently. "And be sure to attend chapel on Sundays. Now you had better go to dinner," she added with a smile. "You look as if you could stand a decent meal."

Dinner was served in a large communal hall where I had the opportunity to meet my fellow students. Most of them were clean-cut young boys from Midwestern towns who were away from home for the first time. The food was good. There was fried chicken, mountains of mashed potatoes, and corn bread, all of which was washed down with large pitchers of ice-cold milk. Dessert consisted of apple pie with vanilla ice cream. I ate everything and decided to take two containers of milk to my room for the night. One could not be sure, after all, if all that milk would last.

My academic adviser, to whom I was introduced the following morning, was the only Jewish faculty member on campus. Professor Joseph Dunner had come to the United States from Germany in 1938, as a refugee from Hitler. He was a thoughtful man with a leonine mane who enjoyed a reputation as somewhat of an eccentric. He taught courses in international politics and advised me to prepare for a career as a political scientist. My background, in his opinion, would equip me ideally for that profession. It would be hard work, he warned.

I enrolled in Professor Dunner's course and quickly looked to him for friendship and guidance. He was a kind and generous man whose marriage was childless and unhappy. Soon, he began to regard me almost like a son. We would take long walks together in the Iowa countryside, where I slowly opened up and told him about my childhood in Europe and China. He listened with sympathy while drawing on his meerschaum pipe. I wondered if my own father would have talked to me like this.

I promised him that I would work hard to become a political scientist, but I would just as readily have promised him I would study astronomy. What I really craved was his affection. It became my ambition to become the best student in the college, and I worked long hours into the night to achieve that goal. Only in that way, I thought, would I be worthy of his love. I needed this father figure. I needed his approval. I wanted to make him as proud of me as I think my father would have been.

I drove myself so hard that, one day, my mentor became quite concerned and said, "You are alone too much, and you work too hard. It's spring and I don't think you have even noticed."

Twice a week, I abandoned my political science texts for a few hours and walked over to the music building. There, in a small cubicle, I would play snatches of Beethoven sonatas for a while. I went not so much to practice as to vent my emotions. While playing, I realized that I wasn't really happy. In fact, I was miserably lonely.

Except for Professor Dunner, I hadn't made any friends. The students were cordial and genuinely friendly, but there was no one like Rusty with whom I could share my feelings and develop a sense of emotional intimacy. Rusty and I exchanged long letters, but it was difficult to bridge the distance between two continents. He was now studying to be an accountant in Australia. The five hundred girls mentioned by Mrs. Hall—some of whom were very pretty, even beautiful—might as well have not been there at all, as I was much too frightened to approach any of them. While playing the piano one night, it occurred to me that I was almost twenty years old and had never even touched a girl.

One spring evening in my second year at school, I heard a knock on the door of my cubicle.

"Come in," I said. I was playing the slow movement of Beethoven's "Pathétique Sonata," feeling maudlin and rather sorry for myself. The door opened and a girl walked in. She had dark hair, had lively and warm brown eyes, and was wearing a close-fitting sweater.

"You play beautifully," the girl said. I felt myself blush.

"Thank you very much," I managed to stammer in my best British public school English. The girl's eyes lit up.

"Aren't you the foreign student from China?" she asked. "I have heard about you," she added, laughing. "They call you the Jewish Chinaman."

I looked at her smiling brown eyes and said nothing. I seemed to have lost the power of speech.

"My name is Julie Stein," the girl said, and sat down on the chair beside me. "Play some more Beethoven."

I walked her home that evening. At the door, she put her arms around my neck and kissed me on the mouth, pressing her body to mine. I began to tremble at the touch of her soft and warm mouth. She disengaged herself and looked at me with eyes that seemed almost liquid.

"There is a chamber music concert tomorrow night," she said. "I am playing the cello. Why don't you come?"

"Of course I will," I promised.

"You look like an artist," she said. Then she kissed me once more and disappeared.

Julie's home was in a large Midwestern city. Her father, she informed me, was a prosperous businessman who had sent her away to college to find a husband. But she preferred artists to businessmen, she said with a laugh, and wasn't ready yet to settle down.

She kissed me again after the concert. This time, she took my hand and placed it gently on her breast. Her heart, I noticed, was racing as wildly as my own. Then she took my head between her hands and looked at me. Her liquid eyes were serious.

"You know, I am a virgin," she said.

"So am I," I blurted out.

Suddenly, we both laughed. Something had happened between us. The awkwardness was gone.

Sunday afternoon, Julie and I rented two bicycles and rode out into the countryside. She had packed a picnic and our destination was a wooded area near a lake, about twenty miles away from the college. Julie wore a light blue spring dress and looked lovely. We raced part of the way and arrived at the little lake breathless and hungry. The picnic area was crowded with students who had taken advantage of the beautiful spring afternoon to escape from their books. We put on our bathing suits and jumped in the water. Then Julie unpacked the picnic basket and we ate.

Later, as it began to get dark, I became concerned. I knew that it would take at least an hour to return to school, and I did not want Julie to get into trouble.

"Shouldn't we go back?" I asked.

"Let's stay a while longer," Julie answered. "It's such a beautiful night."

Suddenly, Julie sat up and said a little brusquely, "Don't move, I'll be right back."

I continued to lie on my back and look up into the night sky. But after a while, I became concerned again and sat up. Julie was nowhere to be seen. I rose and walked to the edge of the lake to look out over the water.

It did not take me long to spot Julie. She was swimming in the middle of the lake, her white arms clearly visible in the moonlight. At the shallow end, she stopped swimming, her body rising slowly out of the water. She was completely nude and looked very beautiful. *This is how Adam must have felt when he saw Eve for the first time,* I thought to myself.

I had lost all fear and walked to the edge of the lake. Julie was out of the water. Wordlessly, we clung to each other. *Love is so simple,* I thought. The silkworm moths I had watched on my windowsill in China flashed through my mind.

"I love you, Julie," I whispered.

"I love you, too," she said.

Afterward, we lay together on the grass, holding hands.

Neither of us spoke much as we bicycled home, and I hated to part from her at the door.

First love.

Each time we were together, the world was born again. Julie's love transformed the most ordinary objects around us into something beautiful. Music, pictures, books, all took on a secret meaning. Clichés and banalities were banished. My life before I had met Julie seemed nothing more than a series of rough, preliminary sketches. I discovered the deep complicity between lovers that excludes everything beyond it. We made the world into our secret garden, and life became a prayer that only Julie's love could grant. When I embraced her, I found a sanctuary beyond the world's perils, a state of grace with pardon granted and justice rendered. It was the first time since Rusty and I had parted that I did not feel alone.

Vienna seemed a million miles away. The Nazis seemed dark, faceless figures in a shattered nightmare. I pushed all of that far into the recesses of my mind and here, in Iowa, I had walked into the light and could start to live. I would prove Oskar wrong.

Commencement was only two months away. I was ranked first in my graduating class and had been admitted to graduate school at Harvard with a scholarship. Professor Dunner beamed with pride. He told me that I had been his best student in many years of teaching. Julie wanted me to marry her and enter her father's business. We had been lovers for more than two years now, and the time had come, she said, to settle down and to have children. I had every reason to be satisfied with my life, yet I was, once again, not happy. While I loved Julie, the idea of marriage terrified me. Besides, Professor Dunner's encouragement had given me a measure of intellectual self-confidence. I had my heart set on Harvard and wanted to prepare myself for a career in the academic world.

One day in early May, Julie complained of nausea and went to the college infirmary for a checkup. Three days later, she appeared at my dormitory white with shock. The college nurse had informed her coldly that she was pregnant and had immediately decided to report her condition to the college dean. An icy terror gripped me. *We had been careful,* I thought, but obviously not careful enough. I comforted Julie as best I could and then went to see my only friend, Professor Dunner.

My mentor heard me out and shook his head. Then he looked at me gravely and said, "You will have to marry her right away and make the best of it."

"What about Harvard?" I asked, and felt my knees going weak under me.

"I don't know," Professor Dunner answered, deep in thought. "We will have to see."

The next morning at ten, I received a call from the office of the college president requesting my presence at noon. My heart was heavy with fear as I walked over to the administration building. An elderly secretary with bluish hair ushered me in. She was a jolly person who usually had a smile for everyone. Today, she did not smile.

I found myself standing before the president. I did not know Dr. Stevens well. He often preached sermons in Sunday chapel and was known to abhor cigarettes and liquor. Now he looked at me with cold gray eyes, his thin lips pressed together in a grim line.

"I will ask you only a single question," Dr. Stevens said as he paced before me with his hands folded behind his back. He paused and came to stop in front of me. "Did you have sexual intercourse with Julie?"

The question rang out like a pistol shot.

"Yes," I said with a nod.

"I am sorry to have to tell you this," Dr. Stevens said, "but you are a rotten apple and I have to take measures to make sure that you don't contaminate the other apples in the barrel."

I looked at him. He did not look the least bit sorry for me.

"I am grieved for you, young man," he continued. "Your academic record here has been outstanding, but that is no excuse for flagrant immorality." He took a deep breath. "I have no alternative but to expel you from the college, effective immediately. You will not be permitted to graduate. You are an alien, and it is my obligation to report this matter to the immigration authorities. What you and Julie do is your own affair." Dr. Stevens paused, seeming to enjoy the pun. "But you will have to leave the college within the next twenty-four hours. That is all."

He had taken off his glasses and begun to polish them with quick, angular movements. His eyes, I noticed, had the look of hard, gray marble.

"I offered him my resignation if he does not let you graduate," Dr. Dunner said. It was the next day and I was sitting in the professor's small garden. "That frightened him," he continued. "He has agreed to mail your diploma to you, but you must be gone from here tomorrow. It was the best I could do with that bastard."

I looked at my mentor gratefully. I had never seen him so enraged, and I noticed with immense relief that his anger was not directed toward me.

"You had better get out of here," Dr. Dunner said gently. "The entire college knows about it."

He rose and we shook hands. Then he looked at me and added with a smile, "I don't think Harvard will mind if this earthshaking scandal should reach Cambridge." As usual, he had read my thoughts.

"Thank you for being a father to me," I said, unable to stop my tears. "I will try to make you proud of me."

"I know you will," Dr. Dunner said.

Julie and I left for St. Louis the next day. Her father welcomed us warmly and did not seem at all perturbed by his daughter's pregnancy. He was a fat little man who liked to smoke large cigars.

"Welcome to the family," he boomed. "I never thought I would have a Jewish Chinaman as a son-in-law. Maybe I'll be blessed with a slant-eyed grandchild." He laughed loudly, savoring his joke.

Julie's mother was in the kitchen trying to feed dozens of relatives who had dropped by to look me over. The wedding date was only a week away and Julie was busy shopping with friends for a wedding gown. In my carpeted guest room, I felt like a prisoner.

Everything happened too fast. I never proposed. It was a foregone conclusion there would be a wedding and it had to happen quickly to save face for her family. I took no part in the planning, as I was frightened and confused by the prospect of becoming a husband and a father. My focus was an education in America and hoping for the dreams that Rusty's mother had envisioned for me. This was not in my plan. I didn't think things could get much worse, but they did.

A few days later, I received a call from the Omaha office of the Immigration and Naturalization Service. An inspector wished to see me immediately.

"We have had a complaint against you on the grounds of moral turpitude," the immigration official began. I was standing in his office as he scratched his crew cut in apparent embarrassment. "We may have to begin deportation proceedings against you," he continued.

A nameless terror rose in my throat.

"Where to?" I managed to croak.

"What was your place of residence before you entered the United States?" the inspector asked in a businesslike tone.

"Shanghai, China."

"Well, we can't very well ship you back," the inspector said after a moment's hesitation. "The commies have taken over there, haven't they?"

I nodded. Mao Tse-tung's army had occupied Shanghai six months ago.

"I guess we will have to deport you to your place of origin. Where were you born?" he asked.

"Vienna, Austria," I said.

The inspector began to scratch his head again.

"Haven't the commies taken over that town, too?" he wanted to know.

"Vienna is divided into four sectors," I replied dutifully, "and one of them is occupied by the Soviet Union."

"And in which sector were you born?" the inspector asked. His voice had become impatient.

I hesitated. I had no idea in which of the four sectors the little house of my birth was located. It was probably a heap of rubble by now anyway.

"In the Russian sector," I said.

"Damn!" The inspector had leaned back in his armchair and was looking at me. I seemed to be causing endless trouble for him. "We can't ship you back into the arms of our enemies after we have paid for your education," he said, scratching his head again. "What the hell is your nationality?" he asked suddenly, his face brightening.

"I have no nationality," I answered truthfully. "The Germans made me into a stateless refugee."

The inspector glared at me. His face had become angry, but then he suddenly began to laugh. He laughed so loudly that he was bellowing.

"Pete," he yelled to a man sitting behind a desk a few feet away. "I don't know what to do with this guy; he is the original man without a country. We may have to invent a country to deport him to."

Pete, an older man with a balding head, shuffled over. "Aren't you supposed to be marrying an American citizen?" he asked.

"Yes," I answered, "the day after tomorrow."

"You had better do it fast," Pete said. Then he turned to the crew cut. "Let him go, Mike," he said. "The boy is about to become a father." Pete winked at me and handed me a cigar. I took it and put it in my pocket.

"Thank you, sir," I said. "Thank you very much."

"You've got a week," said Pete. Mike scratched his head, saying nothing. He was still scratching when I walked out the door.

The wedding was a large and noisy affair and I went through it like a stone. In a haze, I listened to a rabbi pronounce the marriage vows and heard myself say, "I do." Then dozens of people I had never seen slapped me on the back and stuffed money into my pockets. I fished out the bills and gave them all to Julie. She looked radiant, but I looked at her as if she were a stranger. I knew she loved me, but all I felt was guilt and terror. What I had loved was the romantic girl who had walked toward me out of the lake. What I saw before me now was a full-grown woman, eager to take on the duties of a wife and mother. But I was still a boy, it seemed, albeit a boy about to become a father.

A heavy hand slapped me on the back. It was Julie's father. He was slightly drunk and out of breath after having danced with Julie. He patted his daughter's belly. "She dances pretty good, the little mother," he said proudly. Then he turned to me and said, "Son, tomorrow morning you come with me to the office. I want to break you in as a future partner. And here is my wedding gift to you—it's a dowry, just like in the old country." He stuffed a piece of paper into my pocket.

Julie smiled at her father, her eyes dancing. "Thank you, Daddy," she said, kissing him on the cheek.

"Thank you, sir," I mumbled. I took the piece of paper out of my pocket. It was a check for ten thousand dollars, made out in my name.

"From now on you will call me Dad," said Julie's father.

On our wedding night, Julie wanted to make love, but my body refused to cooperate. *At least that part of me is honest,* I thought in self-disgust. I was afraid of Julie, afraid to tell her the truth: that I did not want to be a partner in her father's business and that instead I yearned to go to Harvard with my scholarship.

"We will have a good life," Julie said lovingly. "I hope we have a son."

I said nothing. All I felt was terrible guilt.

I didn't want to be a husband and I didn't want a child. I had agreed to marry Julie because I had no choice. Suddenly I was gripped with a violent urge to kill myself, to slash my wrists, my throat, anything to stop this guilt, this pain. The memory of Papa flooded through me. *Perhaps suicide is easy for those who have it in the family,* I thought. It seemed like a natural thing to do, almost like walking from one room to another, far from the complex theories I had read about in psychology texts at school. Despair, self-hatred, and hopelessness, I thought, were quite enough. I was a child of suicide: I would kill myself and join Papa. At last, the dream would have a happy ending. I would see his face again.

Julie had fallen asleep. I got out of bed, put on my clothes, and left the house. I walked along the banks of the Mississippi River, looking for a place to jump. Twice I took a running leap and stopped just in time. Despite my despair, I was beginning to feel ridiculous. I suspected that, even if I jumped, I would probably try to swim to safety. Instead of yet another try, I reached into my pocket to blow my nose and felt a piece of paper. It was the check for ten thousand dollars made out to me by Julie's father. I looked at it for a long time, then slowly tore it into several small pieces that I threw into the water.

Dawn was breaking when I returned to the house. Julie was awake when I walked in. She was frantic with worry. We were to leave for a monthlong honeymoon that afternoon.

"Where on earth have you been?" she asked, her eyes searching mine.

"Please sit down," I said. My voice must have carried a new authority. She obeyed without a word.

"Julie," I said, "I will not be a partner in your father's business. I have torn up the check and thrown it into the Mississippi. I will go to Harvard. If you come with me, I will do my best to make our marriage work, but if you don't, I will go alone."

Julie's eyes became dark. For a long time, she said nothing.

"I will go alone, then," I repeated.

"You are crazy, completely mad," she said.

"Look here," I implored, reaching for her hand. "If I am unhappy, I shall make you and the child unhappy, too."

Julie began to cry. "You are throwing away your life," she sobbed. "Here you have a family, I love you as I will never love another man, and Dad already looks at you as if you were his son. He always wanted a son," she sobbed hysterically. "Someday you will take over his business. What is it that you want that we can't give you?"

"I don't want to be a businessman," I answered miserably.

"Go to your damn Harvard then," Julie screamed at the top of her voice. Her eyes had become wild with despair. "I thought you loved me!"

"I did," I answered truthfully.

"And now?" Julie looked at me, her liquid eyes imploring me.

"Of course I love you," I lied, reaching for her hand.

We then made love awkwardly, almost like two strangers. *How can feelings shift so quickly?* I thought to myself. Two hours ago, I was close to suicide and now I was having sex with my bride. It occurred to me that if sex could make me feel that much better, I was certainly not ready to kill myself. Or perhaps I was enjoying it because I had dared to be more honest. I didn't really know. Later, we fell asleep in each other's arms.

Toward noon, there was a knock at our bedroom door.

It was Julie's father.

"Time to show you the business," he said through the door. "I have changed your tickets so that you can leave on your honeymoon tomorrow."

"Thank you, sir," I said, "but I am not going."

"Okay, take your time," Julie's father replied. I heard him laugh as he went down the stairs.

I looked at Julie.

"Are you still going?" she asked.

"Yes," I said. Nothing had changed. Julie watched in silence as I packed my few belongings.

"You really are crazy," she repeated. It was like a rerun of the earlier scene.

"I probably am," I agreed.

Suddenly, I felt a surge of strength course through my body. For the first time in my life, I no longer felt quite so helpless. The guilt was still there, but it was no longer crushing me. As I said good-bye, Julie jumped out of bed and ran toward me.

"I will be waiting for you here when you come to your senses," she whispered softly, putting her arms around me.

"I will not come to my senses," I replied.

Then I walked out the door and crept noiselessly past the living room. I was afraid to run into Julie's father. *I am still a goddamn coward,* I said to myself. *But maybe I can learn.* Then I made my way to the bus terminal. Three hours later, I was on a Greyhound bus heading east for Boston.

I gazed out the window at the flatlands rushing by. A heavy sadness weighed upon me. If Julie had supported my wish to learn and grow, our love might have endured. Together, we might have overcome the trauma of the shotgun marriage. If only she had come with me to Harvard, or even spontaneously offered to, all might have been well. Now it would never be the same.

Love dies when lovers fashion cages for each other. The bars are their own needs. I was alone again. Perhaps we survive, I thought, not only by what we learn, but also by what we manage to forget.

CHAPTER 6

Harvard, 1954

I took a ten-dollar bill out of my pocket and handed it to Mrs. Hersey. The old landlady slowly climbed the stairs of the little wooden house, all the way to the attic.

"This room is ten dollars a week," she said. "Two weeks' rent in advance."

"Fine," I said, and gave her another ten-dollar bill.

"The bathroom is one flight below," Mrs. Hersey added, "and there is a pay telephone on the street corner." She folded the two bills carefully and wrote out a receipt. "Do you have any more luggage?" she asked.

I shook my head. "That's it," I answered, pointing to the two bags I had carried up the stairs.

Mrs. Hersey hesitated a moment. "There is a laundry two blocks away," she said. "They give you one-day service there." Then she shuffled out and closed the door.

The room was hot and stuffy. I opened the window and looked out on a row of wooden houses, the sight of which I found depressing. I decided to take a walk and think over my situation.

I had been so eager to get to Harvard that I arrived almost three months early with less than fifty dollars to my name. It was late

June now, and I had no place else to go and was practically broke. I would have to find a job not only to last the summer, but also to save some money for September as well. The scholarship money wouldn't be enough for room and board during the academic year.

A young boy near Harvard Square was selling newspapers and seemed to be doing a brisk business. I bought a paper and looked at the headline: AGGRESSION IN KOREA, it proclaimed in bold, red ink. *There is no end to it,* I thought as I walked through Harvard Yard. Only five years after Hiroshima, young men would again be dying. I felt a surge of helplessness and rage. Perhaps I should not have torn up that check after all. Perhaps Julie's father had been right. "Look after your wife and kid," he had said, "and let the rest of the world go to hell." I thought of Julie and missed her soft, warm body. *Maybe she, too, had been right,* I thought. *Maybe I really was crazy.*

I stopped in front of a small luncheonette with a COUNTERMAN WANTED sign in the window. *Why not?* I thought, opened the door, and sat down at the counter. A little man with a jet-black handlebar mustache darted back and forth behind the counter.

"One cheeseburger, heavy on the french fries," he yelled into the kitchen.

"Come on, Charlie, I ordered that burger ten minutes ago," grunted a man with enormous buttocks that were spilling down over the counter stool.

"What will it be?" Charlie said, ignoring the disgruntled man and wiping off the counter in front of me.

"I want the job," I replied. Charlie stopped wiping and looked up.

"Forty bucks a week plus tips and lunch," he said. "Eight hours a day. You can start right now."

"Okay," I said, "give me an apron."

I lasted at Charlie's less than two weeks. The work was hard and tips were meager. After lunch, when the rush was over, Charlie made us wash the dishes and clean the floor. For lunch he permitted only spaghetti and two meatballs. Absalom, the black cook, began to feel sorry for me and regularly hid two more meatballs under the spaghetti. Thus, every day at three o'clock, I carried a mountain of spaghetti topped with the two visible meatballs past Charlie's watchful eye. On one occasion, for some unknown reason, Charlie became suspicious.

"Hold it," he commanded suddenly as I was carrying my lunch plate to the far end of the counter. He took a fork and poked around in the spaghetti. It did not take long to discover the contraband at the bottom of the plate. Charlie looked at me and made a lightning calculation.

"Two extra meatballs at a quarter a piece for ten days make five dollars even," he said authoritatively, holding out his hand.

I reached into my pocket and handed him a five-dollar bill. Taking off my apron, I thought desperately for some particularly brilliant parting insult to throw in his face. None occurred to me. Absalom had come out of the kitchen and was grinning behind Charlie's back. He held up two fingers in a victory sign. *He must have been a soldier in the war,* I thought as I closed the door behind me.

I eventually made my way to the headquarters of the Check Protection Corporation in downtown Boston. Charlie's pride had been a check-writing machine that he had installed next to the cash register. The machine imprinted each check with Charlie's name and perforated the amounts for which the checks were written. "Protects me against forgery," Charlie had declared proudly.

One afternoon, a salesman had come in to service the machine. He had left me his card.

"There is good money to be made with these machines," he said. "Each sale means a profit of a hundred dollars. When you get tired of this dumb job, come and see us."

And so I did.

"It's hard work," said Steve, the chief of the firm's sales force. I had come to his office to discuss employment at the Check Protection Corporation, and he had just explained the basic pitch to me. It consisted of going door-to-door with a sample machine, demonstrating its virtues and appealing to the prospective buyer's ego and his fear: the personal nameplate was for the ego and the perforator was for the fear. The top salesmen pitched about thirty businesses a day and averaged about ten sales a week. Each sale meant a net profit of eighty dollars. If I could sell one machine a day for the rest of the summer, I calculated, the profits would see me through the first year of graduate school.

After a week's apprenticeship, I was ready and walked into the office of a lobster retailer on the south Boston wharf.

"Sir," I said tentatively to the owner, "have you heard that there have been a lot of check forgeries lately in this neighborhood?"

The man looked up. He was wearing rubber gloves and sorting lobsters. "No," he said, "I haven't."

"Sir," I continued in a businesslike tone, "do you mail your checks?"

"Sure, that's normal business procedure, isn't it?"

"Let me show you what risks you run," I said gravely, pulling out a recent issue of the *Boston Globe*. On the front page were two men in handcuffs who had been arrested for check forgery.

"Do you know what these men did?" I asked. The man shook his head. He had taken off his rubber gloves. I took a specimen check out of my pocket.

"Write down your signature," I said. The man looked up hesitantly.

"Don't worry, I will tear it up in a minute," I promised. "Now give me one of your business envelopes." He handed me an envelope.

"Now watch me," I said as I took out a pair of knitting needles and inserted them into the airhole of the envelope. Grasping the check between the needles, I rolled it up inside the sealed envelope and slowly pulled it out through the airhole.

"By the way, may I have your name, sir?" I said politely.

"Fish," said the man. I looked at him incredulously.

"That's right, Barrington Fish," he repeated.

"Now watch me copy your signature," I continued. I had learned that almost any signature could be reproduced by placing the original upside down and copying it backward. I managed a fair facsimile of Mr. Fish's signature.

By now I had his rapt attention.

"They get a hold of your mail," I said, "then they extract the check and study your signature. They put the check back in and allow it to reach its proper destination. But two or three weeks later, they cash checks with your signature, and by the time you find out about it, they are gone and you are out of a lot of money."

I stopped a moment and took out the sample check writer.

"How much is this goddamn thing?" asked Mr. Fish.

"One hundred fifty dollars," I replied.

"I'll take it," said the lobsterman. "I will write you the check on the machine."

We concluded the transaction and shook hands, thereby earning me eighty dollars in less than twenty minutes. During the next two months, I sold an average of one machine a day.

Steve had been right, though. It was grueling work, and most of the time I did not get much past the door. One afternoon, I decided to ring the bell of a funeral parlor. A pale-faced man with slicked-down hair led me to an adjacent ice-cold room smelling of formaldehyde.

"Mr. Santori," said the man to a figure bent over a large table, "a salesman is here to see you."

"Well?" asked Santori impatiently. I noticed that he was injecting fluid into what appeared to be a corpse. "I am embalming this man," Santori said, noticing my look. "If you want to sell me something, you will have to watch."

Halfway through my pitch, Santori waved his hand and interrupted. "I don't write any checks," he declared imperiously. "All my business is done in cash."

"You mean you send cash through the mail?" I asked, making a last effort.

"No," Santori replied, "I don't use the mail, either."

"No checks, no mail?" I said, my courage fading fast.

"That's right," Santori said. "I don't trust banks, I don't trust the mail; and I certainly don't trust you." He had finished his embalming work and was slowly coming toward me.

"I am sorry," I said quickly, backing out the door. "I am sorry to have bothered you."

By Labor Day, I had saved up almost three thousand dollars. Students were beginning to come into town and filled up the rooming houses near the university. I discovered happily that my diploma from Grinnell had been received in good order, proof that Professor Dunner had kept his word. I had not had word from Julie, but by this time, I had learned that Oskar and my mother had fled China and were settled in New York. When I went to register for classes, the dean congratulated me on my scholarship.

"You did a great job out there at Grinnell," he said. "We are happy to have you here at Harvard." Then he held out his hand to me and smiled.

My fellow students, whom I met at mealtimes during the next few days, were a small but formidable group. One was a brilliant Polish Catholic named Zbigniew Brzezinski who was engrossed in Stalin's bloody purges. He had a quick and powerful intelligence, buttressed by a touch of playful cruelty toward those who were not armed with his extraordinary gift for repartee. A conversation with him tended to resemble a barrage of staccato-like artillery fire. An impish face beneath a shock of unruly blond hair gave "Zbig" the appearance of a high school boy, but I seldom saw anyone get the better of him.

I also befriended Stanley Hoffman, an Austrian-born but Sorbonne-educated intellectual through and through. He was endowed with a charming Gallic wit that masked a basic shyness and carefully guarded sense of privacy.

Then there was George Liska, who had fled from the Communists in Prague, and cut an elegant but remote figure that reminded me of a medieval cardinal. Kafka-like and melancholy, he often spoke in riddles and tended toward solitude.

Samuel Huntington, a native-born American, was studying the relationship between the soldier and the state. To the amazement of most of us, he suggested that America had more to learn from West Point than West Point from America.

All of us believed that the atomic bomb had changed our world forever. Most of us looked at the study of history with impatience and suspicion. The past could not help us much, we thought.

There was one anomaly in our midst. We had heard that a senior at Harvard College had submitted a 377-page undergraduate honors thesis, modestly titled "The Meaning of History." Rumor had it that Professor William Elliott had read the first one hundred pages and awarded the young senior summa cum laude. This aroused our interest and envy for several reasons. In the first place, summa cum laude was extremely rare and exempted the fortunate recipient from the dreaded oral examination for the doctorate; second, we were struck by the content of the thesis: this undergraduate had dared to take on Spengler, Toynbee, and Kant. Finally, and most incomprehensibly, this bachelor of arts had apparently announced his intention to write a doctoral thesis for the Department of Government on the diplomacy of the early nineteenth century. Our curiosity was aroused even further since none of us had ever met the author of "The Meaning of History." The young man had a reputation for brooding in the stacks of Widener Library while we were discussing the latest events on the world scene. But one day, in early October 1950, he joined us at our lunchroom table. That was when I first met Henry Kissinger.

Kissinger was several years older than most of us and seemed austere and rather distant. His close-cropped hair gave him a stern military look. I had heard that he was a Jewish refugee from Germany and that he had served as a sergeant in the occupation of his homeland. Inevitably, the conversation drifted to the subject of his dissertation. He was interested in the problem of peace, Kissinger explained, and because of this, the Congress of Vienna of 1815 had attracted his attention. The challenges of those distant days struck him as analogous to those of our time. We were astounded. Had he not heard of the atom bomb? someone asked. What could Metternich and Castlereagh possibly teach us? Brzezinski smiled and suggested that Kissinger might wish to transfer to the history department. Kissinger, totally unruffled, rose from the table and got himself another helping of chicken à la king.

What impressed me most about Henry Kissinger during that luncheon discussion was his self-assurance and intellectual power. He argued forcefully and brilliantly. It did not seem to me, however, as I listened, that he was particularly interested in impressing or converting anyone around him. It seemed almost as if he were carrying on a dialogue with himself rather than with his interlocutors. We did not quite know what to make of him; there was something puzzling about him, yet one could sense a fierce ambition.

Kissinger left the table when he completed his exposition. The rest of us immediately discussed his thesis. Someone asked under which professor Kissinger was planning to work. It turned out that William Elliott had agreed to continue as his mentor. Elliott was one of the two most powerful professors in the government department. The other was Carl J. Friedrich. Both men taught political philosophy and were bitter intellectual rivals, and all doctoral students found out soon after arriving that they had to make a choice between the two—it was apparently impossible to be on cordial terms with both. Perhaps the most remarkable thing about Henry Kissinger, most of us thought, was the fact he had managed to be on excellent terms with both these supreme rivals of the Harvard government department. Not without envy, I wondered how he managed that. No one knew the answer.

Henry Kissinger and his wife, Ann, lived in a small apartment near the university. Ann was a shy, attractive girl who, like her husband, had fled from Nazi Germany. She seemed to be content to live in Kissinger's shadow and seldom spoke much in his presence. Once, when I rang their doorbell on a Sunday afternoon, Ann opened the door and put her finger to her mouth.

"Talk softly," she said, "Henry is thinking."

After a while, he emerged from his study, still deep in thought.

"Castlereagh's suicide was a tragedy for Metternich," he said to no one in particular, taking off his glasses. "Metternich lost his one dependable friend."

I nodded. I didn't really know much about Metternich, but I admired Henry's single-minded dedication to his work, even though it frightened me a little. It was always the same with him: whatever preoccupied him at the moment would become the subject of our conversation. I quickly recognized that Kissinger's ambitions ranged far beyond the academic world and that he would let nothing stop him.

There was about Kissinger a sense of brooding melancholy. The past somehow always hovered over him. I knew, of course, about his youth as a Jew in Nazi Germany and his escape, barely in time, from the coming Holocaust. He knew my similar history, but we seldom talked about it, partially out of fear of causing the other anguish from the painful memories, but also because Kissinger tended to withdraw when the conversation became personal.

"The past is dead," he told me once. "I am interested in the future." I was deeply drawn to him and he, too, sought me out.

"You are a good friend," he would often say to me. And yet, when I would try to talk about emotions rather than our intellectual or professional pursuits, the barriers went up. In the end, although I recognized his genius, I sometimes felt lonely in his presence.

If Kissinger had a mentor, it was another Jewish refugee from Germany. Professor Hans J. Morgenthau, almost a generation older than most of us, had just published a major work in world politics that was to become the leading classic in the field. Not surprisingly, Morgenthau's vision of the world was a tragic one. It rejected the facile belief in progress and the rationality of man that had been typical of most American thinkers. Instead, he advanced a "realist theory," which regarded the struggle for power as the persistent essence of international relations everywhere. Morgenthau taught a seminar at Harvard as a visiting professor and most of us attended. I, too, was attracted by his uncompromising honesty and intellectual daring. His deeply pessimistic lectures were laced with a brilliant and mordant wit that was very similar to Kissinger's own. On one occasion, an eager, somewhat unsophisticated student wanted to know whether the United Nations was being faithful to the ideals of its charter. "The count of Hesse Coburg was once asked whether he had been faithful to his wife," Morgenthau replied, "and he answered, 'Sometimes.'"

Across the hallway from the Kissingers lived my mentor, Inis Claude, and his wife, Marie. I had been too timid to approach either Elliott or Friedrich and had instead befriended this young instructor who taught a course on the United Nations. Claude was a first-rate lecturer and quickly managed to rouse my interest in the new world organization. Soon he made me his assistant and suggested that I write a doctoral thesis on the world refugee problem. Over dinner at his home, Claude would be a kind and gentle critic of my work while Marie would listen quietly, sewing a woolen shirt for me.

Sometimes Kissinger would drop by and the conversation would shift abruptly from refugees and the United Nations to the theories of Oswald Spengler. On one such occasion, another young instructor who was a dinner guest tried to steer the conversation to academic politics. Kissinger glared at him.

"You are wasting energy," he declared contemptuously. "The fights among academics are so dirty because the stakes are so low." The young instructor fell silent and left shortly afterward, hardly able to conceal his rage. Kissinger seemed quite unaware that he had insulted the young man. He had simply decided that the conversation was a waste of time.

"Everyone should read Spengler," Kissinger said, returning to his favorite topic. "The president could benefit from reading him. I think I shall bring *The Decline of the West* to his attention." Inis Claude and I exchanged a glance. "I think I will send it to the president," he muttered to himself with a small smile.

When I returned home that evening, a letter was waiting for me. It was from Julie. "We have a son," she wrote. "I am ready to try and live with you in Cambridge." There was a postscript below her signature. "We will have to live on your income," it said. "Daddy never wants to talk to you again."

"May I have another piece of chicken?" I asked Julie. We were having dinner in the kitchenette of our two-room flat, a year after she had moved in with me at Cambridge. The baby had finally stopped crying and was sleeping in his crib.

Julie shook her head. "I bought only two chicken legs," she said. "I was short of cash again."

I looked into the empty pot and then at Julie. *This can't go on,* I thought, desperate. Ever since I had assumed responsibility for her and the child, my studies had suffered grievously. I was selling check writers again, and on weekends I helped a local rabbi with his correspondence. Afternoons were taken up with seminars. This left evenings and nights for work on my dissertation, which had to be defended before the end of the semester. I was totally exhausted, yet sleep was a major luxury since the baby cried incessantly. There was neither time nor privacy for anything. My first romance had turned into a sour marriage.

"Julie," I said quietly one evening, "I think you had better go home or we will either kill each other or go crazy."

Julie looked at me with her beautiful liquid eyes. "Make love to me," she said simply.

I looked at her with surprise and felt a sudden wave of tenderness come over me. I led her to our little bed and there we loved each other silently so as not to wake our little boy. When it was over, we both cried. Then we fell asleep, holding on to one another.

I left early the next morning with my sample case, Julie kissing me good-bye at the door. I sold a machine to the owner of a filling station and bought a pint of ice cream on the way home. When I entered the little flat, Julie was nowhere to be seen and the crib was empty. Then I saw the note on the kitchen table.

"I am leaving while we still love each other," it said. "If you want to contact me, I will be with Daddy."

I sat down at the kitchen table, numb with shock. I had begun to feel attached to my little son, and for a long time I stared at the empty crib. Then it occurred to me that Julie had been right to leave. I probably would not have had the courage to leave a second time. As I sat there, I thought of the girl whom I had loved long ago in the summer silence. I sat for a very long time, frozen and waiting for the pain.

About fifty students were sitting around the little foyer in Memorial Hall. Some had taken out their textbooks and had begun to read. Others were chatting or fidgeting impatiently on their chairs. One couple had retired into a corner near the fireplace, where the boy was kissing his girl's ear. It was past nine o'clock and we had been waiting for more than half an hour for the appearance of the little-known Welsh poet who was to give a reading from his latest verses.

In no mood to work on my dissertation, I had taken the evening off. Ever since Julie had left six months earlier, I had been working at a furious pace. In my spare time, I sold machines so I could send Julie money for the support of our son. But tonight I was exhausted. Besides, I rationalized, Friday night was not a good time to sell people check-writing machines. I loved Dylan Thomas's poetry and had come early to get a seat near the front. It had not been difficult since the room was far from crowded. But now I was beginning to get anxious. Perhaps the poet would not appear at all. It was known that he had cancelled many times without apparent reason. This would be one of his last appearances before he died, as I recall.

Suddenly, I heard the shuffling of feet outside the door. Three men walked in side by side, pressed very closely together. Two of them were wearing impeccably pressed clothes, striped ties, and button-down shirts. The well-groomed men were holding up the third between them, whom I recognized instantly as Dylan Thomas. The poet wore a rumpled suit that hung on him like a potato sack. Holding on to the arms of the two young men, he walked unsteadily to the lectern. "He is drunk," I heard a student say in an audible whisper. A slight titter ran through the waiting crowd as the poet fumbled in his pockets and clumsily took out some notes. Then he waited silently for the commotion to subside. *My God,* I thought, my romantic image crumbling, *he looks exactly like a tired salesman.*

Dylan Thomas gazed at us with a look that struck me as reproachful. "You know who I am," it seemed to say, "so why do you humiliate me?" Then he bent his tousled head over his notes and began to read. At once, the room fell absolutely silent. I realized again that, imprisoned in this shapeless body dwelt the spirit of poetic genius. His rich, sonorous voice enveloped us in cadences that sounded more like music than the spoken word. Time seemed suspended. "And you, my father, there on the sad height," the poet read, "Curse, bless, me now with your fierce tears, I pray. Do not go gentle into that good night. Rage, rage against the dying of the light. . . ."

"Thank you," Dylan Thomas said after a pause, and stuffed his notes back into his pockets.

After an all-too-brief performance, there was a loud and sustained round of applause. The poet smiled for the first time and his face suddenly appeared almost boyish. Then he stepped away from the lectern, which had seemed much too high for him, and walked quickly to the door. His step was firm now and there was no trace of unsteadiness. At the door he smiled again and waved his arm in a gesture of farewell. The applause seemed to have buoyed his spirits. Two minutes later he was gone.

Two months later, I received my doctorate. Commencement became a memorable occasion when the lieutenant who had gotten me the admission to Grinnell showed up during the academic procession to surprise me. Deeply touched, I shined his shoes one last time in gratitude. Since no shoe-shining cloth was readily available to provide polish, my academic gown came to the rescue. We hugged and promised to stay in touch. It was not to be, however. A few months later, my benefactor succumbed to a fatal heart attack.

Inis Claude walked over from the academic procession and shook my hand warmly. There was a teaching job open in New York, he said. Was I interested?

"Yes," I said, without a moment's hesitation. Claude looked at me, surprised.

"You should think it over for a week," he admonished gently.

"You are right," I answered, grateful. But I knew I'd accept the job. Two days later, I took the train to New York City.

My relationship with Julie had waned, and I would have little contact with her during this time. Julie remarried. My son would grow up without me.

CHAPTER 7

New York City, 1962

B ennett Cerf, one of the founders of Random House, accompanied me to the Bancroft Awards in 1962. That day, I walked out onto the stage of the large rotunda of Columbia University in my new tuxedo. Dr. Grayson Kirk, the president, was waiting for me at the rostrum, holding a plaque in one hand and an envelope in the other.

"We are proud to honor you today," he said to me, "for having written *The Might of Nations*, the finest book on international relations published in the year 1962." Dr. Kirk handed me the plaque and warmly shook my hand. "The Bancroft Prize is one of the most generous awards in the academic world," he declared, facing the audience. "It carries an award of four thousand dollars." He smiled and handed me the envelope. I looked out over the five hundred elegant, applauding people who had braved an April rainstorm to come out and honor me.

"Thank you, Mr. President," I managed to say. My voice, I knew, was none too steady. I had decided to make my acceptance speech as short as possible. The reason was that I felt like an imposter or, even worse, a fraud.

In 1963, I was thirty-six and a tenured professor at a leading liberal arts college in New York City. I was a popular teacher who enjoyed a solid reputation as a scholar and, in addition, was in wide demand as a lecturer all over the United States. My relations with my colleagues at the college were generally good. My income was more than sufficient to meet my needs, especially since Julie had married a wealthy St. Louis pharmacist. I had rented a spacious bachelor apartment on Central Park overlooking the reservoir and had even bought a grand piano. Oskar had died of a malignancy on his adrenal gland the year before and my mother had opened a tiny millinery store on upper Broadway. My health was excellent and I enjoyed regular tennis at a private club within walking distance of my home. On weekends, I generally drove my new convertible into the countryside. To all appearances, I was a happy and successful man. The truth was that I felt bored and miserable.

I had climbed the rungs of the academic ladder with unusual speed and realized, not without anxiety, that there were no more promotions to be had. From now on, I would have to set my own standards for my work; any satisfaction would have to flow from its inherent value rather than from a committee of professors passing judgment on my tenure or promotion. I had just published a prize-winning book and the thought of beginning the agonizing chore of writing another frightened me. Even the notion of teaching the same college courses for the next twenty or thirty years made me uneasy.

I enviously watched my colleagues marry and have children as I carried on numerous affairs. Frequently, I led a double or even triple life, the lies and deceptions that were the necessary consequence angering and exhausting me. Yet my fear of loneliness was so intense that I was seldom able to break off a relationship. Usually, a woman would abandon me when she realized that I would not marry her. Each separation then was like an echo of some distant pain. Yet, it was preferable to the prospect of a mediocre marriage.

One such separation caused me considerable anguish. I had become involved with the daughter of Professor Sigmund Neumann, a refugee from Nazi Germany whom I admired greatly for his intellect and generosity and who had gotten me my first job in academe. Eva had fallen in love with me, but I discovered that, although I was already in my thirties, I still yearned to be a son and was terrified of being an adult. In the end, I hurt Eva horribly. It was becoming clear to me that my father's suicide and my tumultuous life had left a gaping, perhaps irreparable, wound.

On one occasion, I became so desperate that I consulted a psychoanalyst. "What would you most like to do with your life?" asked the doctor, not unreasonably.

"Start all over again!" I blurted out, completely truthfully.

The doctor shook his head. "Middle age has hit you early," he said gravely. "Apparently you cannot tolerate success. Be careful that you don't destroy what you have built."

"How often would I have to come and see you?" I inquired.

"Five times a week, for at least three years," the doctor said.

"And what is the cost per session?"

"Eighty dollars," was the answer.

"That's a lot of time and money," I said, rising from my chair.

"It's a bargain," said the doctor, accompanying me to the door.

In the end, I found another outlet that relieved my boredom and frustration. The commodities futures market was a highly speculative vehicle that thrilled me in a way that my love affairs no longer did. While the stock market did not move fast enough to satisfy my need for action, and straight casino gambling struck me as a bore, the markets in cocoa, soybeans, and silver were highly volatile, and a speculator was only required to deposit a margin of 10 percent of the cost of a given futures contract. This made for enormous leverage and lightning action, and if one was on the right side of the market, it was quite possible to pyramid a small investment into a modest fortune. If, on the other hand, one had calculated or guessed wrongly, one could expect a margin call before the trading day had run its course.

The fact that more than 90 percent of all speculators in commodities were known to be losers in the end only increased my sense of challenge; after all, my expertise in international relations would surely give me a decisive edge over the ordinary gambler.

I decided to concentrate on cocoa, which was grown primarily in Ghana and Nigeria. I spent long hours studying crop reports, price trends, and the economic policies of Kwame Nkrumah, Ghana's charismatic president. I read the annual reports of leading candy-bar manufacturers in the United States and studied the chocolate-eating habits of adolescents in the Western Hemisphere. Finally, on the basis of several weeks' exhaustive study, I became convinced that a bull market in cocoa was in the offing. Depositing ten thousand dollars in a margin account at a leading brokerage house, I purchased ten cocoa futures contracts.

Almost immediately after my decision, cocoa prices began to rise. Every day, the value of my contracts rose appreciably. I decided to pyramid, and bought ten more contracts with the profits without having to put up any additional deposit. In less than four weeks, I had parlayed my original investment into almost fifty thousand dollars. My confidence in my newfound talent became contagious. Even my broker began to ask for my advice and listened with respect to what I had to say about crop prospects in Ghana.

One day, however, my broker called. "Cocoa's down the limit," he said glumly.

"What the hell is going on?" I asked, not particularly pleased, even if the cocoa market was entitled to a small correction after its spectacular rise.

"It's been raining unexpectedly in Ghana," the broker said in a knowledgeable tone, "and they think the crop may be larger than expected."

"Who is 'they'?" I asked, more irritably.

"I don't know," he answered, "I guess 'they' are the weather people."

So that was it. I had omitted the weather factor from my calculations, but I decided that this was not an insuperable problem. I remembered that a former student had recently returned to Accra, Ghana, and was working there for a large industrial concern. I had fortunately kept his address and promptly dispatched a cable in which I inquired whether, for a modest sum, he would telegraph daily weather forecasts from the best available local meteorological sources. "Yes," came the immediate reply. Now I would have some firsthand knowledge of the weather in the Ghana cocoa jungles, and I confidently looked forward to the next day's market opening.

At seven o'clock, a cable arrived from Accra. "Rain stopped," it said, "dry weather forecast for next three days." I chuckled to myself. Obviously, the climb of cocoa prices would now resume in earnest. Maybe there would even be a drought. Impatiently, I waited for the phone to ring. It did, at nine o'clock, one hour before the New York opening.

"Cocoa's down again in London," my broker said gloomily. "They are expecting another limit down move in New York."

"But it stopped raining in Ghana!" I shouted into the telephone. "How the hell can cocoa be down?"

"They say it's liquidation by disappointed speculators taking profits," he said.

"Who the hell is 'they'?" I screamed.

"The chartists," he said, and hung up the phone.

When I wasn't in class or preparing for class, I spent the next two weeks in the office of a chart technician named Sam. "Fundamentals do not govern the market exclusively," he instructed me. "You have to study price movements in order to project future trends." Sam adjusted his eyeshade and spread out a huge chart with blue, red, and green lines crossing and crisscrossing each other in complex geometric patterns. "Don't worry," he continued, "my chart indicates a triple bottom for cocoa just about here." He pointed to a spot on his chart not much lower than my purchase price. "It's most unlikely to go lower."

I looked at Sam gratefully. My profits had been wiped out during the last two weeks due to the fierce leverage that was now working in reverse. Worse than that, my confidence was badly shaken. But I was sure that Sam's charted triple bottom would not let me down.

With new hope, I waited for the next trading day. At nine o'clock, unable to wait any longer, I called up my broker.

"What does it look like?" I asked, my heart pounding.

"Down the limit again," he said flatly.

"What about the triple bottom?" I shrieked in a falsetto voice.

"Going through it like a knife through butter. You have a ten-thousand-dollar margin call," he added.

"Sell the goddamn cocoa," I screamed into the telephone, even though I didn't have the money to meet the call. In fact, I was virtually wiped out. My ten thousand dollars had shrunk to a pittance of less than seven hundred.

"I advise that you place a stop order twenty points down," Sam said. "There should be resistance at just about that point."

"Okay," I said, my hope rising again. Surely, the resistance point and the triple bottom would not utterly betray me. At ten o'clock, the phone rang. It was Sam.

"You're out," he said. "They went for the stops."

"Who are 'they'?" I shouted into the phone, choked with rage.

"I don't know," Sam replied a bit unsteadily. "They say it's the large cocoa dealers."

Even though I had been totally wiped out, I still called Sam the next morning. "At least let it go down some more," I prayed. Then I could tell myself that I had done right to sell.

"How's cocoa?" I asked Sam, trying to sound indifferent.

"Up the limit," Sam said quietly. The pain that shot through me was so excruciating that I banged down the telephone. Not only had my money gone into the pocket of some anonymous cocoa trader, but my ego was in tatters. I suddenly realized that I knew absolutely nothing, that if I had done the opposite of what my calculations told me, I would now be rich. And, worse than that, I knew that I was unable to let go, that I was hooked. It was the "rush" of the risk I had first experienced while learning to gamble with the men on the USS *General Gordon*.

Whenever I went broke trading cocoa or some other commodity, I purged myself by writing yet another book. At times, I would write all night long to meet a publisher's deadline. Then when the book was finished, I would become depressed and bored again and soon the unhappy cycle would start anew. Then I would immerse myself in the latest forecasts about the bacon-eating habits of Americans or the supplies of silver bullion in the mint in Washington. Most of the time, I experienced defeat.

Only once, for a brief moment, did I taste an elusive victory. For many months there had been a widespread rush to buy silver as a hedge against inflation. The speculative fever had become so pervasive that brokers virtually pushed one into silver futures— even the elevator operator in my building had decided to invest in silver coins. I sensed that this could not go on forever, and so

I went short. It so happened that I was lucky and had hit the top, the market having broken sharply for several weeks and allowing me to amass a fair amount of money. That short-lived triumph gave me greater pleasure than did the royalty checks earned by my books. Shortly afterward, however, I lost most of the silver profits in soybeans.

But I now saw that the only time I really beat the system—even if only temporarily—was when I ignored everyone around me and walked straight into the tunnel of my fear. I also knew that my gambling had little, if anything, to do with a desire to get rich. Money was simply a way of keeping score, a way of knowing concretely whether I was doing well. The action was the thing I craved. Without it, I felt anxious and empty, as if a vital link to life itself had been cut off. I was dimly beginning to perceive the awful truth: what was keeping me alive was also killing me.

Strangely enough, my work did not suffer in those years. I had become a well-known scholar and my books were used as texts on many college campuses. My classes at the college were always filled, and I genuinely liked my students and my colleagues. I had also developed a repertory of public lectures. My reputation was growing and demand for me was steadily increasing.

The book for which I had received the Bancroft Prize had grown out of my life experience. During the first twenty years of my life in Europe and in China, I had been witness to historical tragedy. And during the second twenty years in the United States, I had come to believe that America was still relatively innocent of tragedy.

Americans—even scholars—generally tended to deny this innocence. They would point to the American Civil War of a century ago, to the Great Depression of the 1930s, and to the two world wars. Perhaps my own experiences had altered my perspective, but it seemed to me that what Americans had experienced on a world level did give the country a unique kind of innocence. When Americans spoke of World War I, I recalled that the combined Anglo-French losses in a single day at the Somme River were greater than America's losses in the entire war, to say nothing of the fact that the war had been waged four thousand miles away from the United States. In World War II, Russia and Germany each lost more men at Stalingrad than America lost in all her wars put together. In China, I had seen abject, grinding poverty and squalor, and when Americans spoke of their Great Depression, I recalled that, in the depression, unemployment had been the crucial problem. But in China, more people were dying of starvation at the time than there were Americans being born in the United States.

And then there was the Holocaust: the murder of six million European Jews, including one million children. *Tragedy* was too weak a word to describe this event. There were simply no words for it, only memory, and for each survivor, his own special hell. For me there were my grandparents, falling into their grave—a mass grave.

The more I studied the United States and the other superpowers, the more I realized that bridges had to be built between them. Each would have to understand the other's history and culture. If we allowed ourselves to be blinded by simpleminded myths and misconceptions, we were doomed. But I began to believe that even understanding was not enough. Nations also had to learn to feel each other with their souls. The other alternative—which I, unlike most Americans, had seen firsthand—was horrendous tragedy, whether it took the form of nuclear war or the terror of a totalitarian regime.

This is where I came to differ with some of my colleagues, and in a very serious manner. The old chessboard power politics had failed and history had moved too quickly. What was needed now was the kind of empathy that flowed from the final knowledge that ultimate tragedy was not only possible, but imminent.

It seemed to me that, as inevitable as historical tragedy appeared to be, there was an inherent paradox in it. If humanity's history appeared as a gigantic river of blood, it was also true that, on the banks of that bloody river, people made love, built houses, and wrote songs, and sometimes children laughed and played. Men had managed to build both cathedrals and concentration camps on the same soil.

It was out of this paradoxical and embattled vision that I began to develop a fascination for the United Nations. Perhaps, in that glass house, people might finally discover that no nation had a monopoly on virtue, justice, or morality. I remembered what I had been taught in school in Austria, Czechoslovakia, and China.

In Vienna I was taught that Austria was the most important nation in the world because, in 1684, an Austrian army had stopped the Turks at the gates of Vienna, thus saving Western civilization. But in Prague, the following year, a Czech teacher had told us that it was a Polish king who had led the decisive charge against the Turks, and that it had been the Slavic peoples who had been the beacon light of history. In Shanghai, a Chinese teacher had informed us that the Middle Kingdom had been the world's fountainhead for several millennia when Europeans and Americans were little better than barbarians. I realized that each country I had lived in exhibited a curious tendency to regard itself as the center of the universe. I even wrote a book on that theme and the United Nations, and to my surprise, the book won considerable critical acclaim.

Despite my success in academic life, however, or perhaps because of it, I was often desperate. The very real recognition I enjoyed made me feel guilty and uncomfortable. It seemed that every upward step I took elicited a countervailing urge to self-destruct. Only when I fell into the pit did I feel cleansed and purged of guilt. It was almost as if someone with enormous power over me had decreed that my life would be an endless cycle between success and self-destruction.

After I had completed my book on the United Nations, my heart was touched again. I had met a woman named Mary Ann Parker who was sitting in the audience at one of my lectures and, attracted by her smile and expressive gray-blue eyes, I asked her out. She took me to her little walk-up flat and played Bach preludes for me. I sensed loneliness in this gentle girl from the South, an almost wordless recognition. We made love that very night and I felt a happiness and a freshness that I had thought were gone forever. In the morning, she prepared breakfast on a little terrace full of flowerpots.

Mary Ann had been born in a little town in northern Arkansas, where her father had been a conductor and her mother a teacher. She had a younger sister, Margaret, whose husband had abandoned her and left her penniless with three young children. Margaret had been unable to pursue her music because of this, despite being a gifted violinist. Mary Ann was herself aspiring to a career in music, but as a concert pianist. She had received a scholarship at a conservatory in New York, and after almost seven years studying there had become estranged from her sister.

One day Mary Ann persuaded Margaret to visit her in New York for a brief stay, and I was invited to join them for an evening at Mary Ann's apartment. As I walked in, I heard the strains of Beethoven's "Spring Sonata" for piano and violin. An emaciated-looking woman stood next to Mary Ann. The sisters played with depth and feeling, but Margaret got stuck in a few places.

"Let it sing, let it sing," Mary Ann encouraged her sister repeatedly. When they had finished, Margaret broke into tears.

"She hasn't touched her fiddle in almost seven years," Mary Ann explained. "But all this is going to change," she added. "I intend to find a job for her in a local orchestra." I was touched and didn't quite know what to do.

"A lot of talent in this family," I said inanely. Margaret looked at me. "Which orchestra did your father conduct?" I asked. The surprise on Margaret's face gave way to puzzlement. Suddenly, Mary Ann began laughing.

"Our father didn't conduct an orchestra," she began.

"But didn't you tell me?" I interrupted.

"He was a conductor on the train to Memphis," Mary Ann explained. The sisters laughed and I laughed with them.

"How about some Mozart?" I asked, and reached for Mary Ann's hand.

I gradually learned to care for Mary Ann, and when she confronted me with an ultimatum of marriage, I found it difficult to leave her. Her presence in my life had become a sanctuary. We made three attempts to get a marriage license, and three times I managed to get sick. Hans Morgenthau, regarded as the Father of Political Science and a world-renowned figure, had been my mentor all these years and became a part of my personal life. I discussed my problem with Professor Morgenthau, who not only urged me to go ahead, but offered to serve as best man at my wedding. In a last, desperate attempt to avoid what I perceived as the marriage trap, I requested an interview with the judge who was to perform the ceremony. The judge, a kindly man, did not take long to notice the state of terror I was in.

"What's your worst fear about marriage?" he asked, looking me straight in the eye.

"I don't think I can promise to 'abandon all others' as prescribed in the wedding vows," I stuttered.

"Why not?" the judge wanted to know.

"Because," I blurted out, "I went through a shotgun marriage once, and it was the worst trauma of my life since coming to America. I was almost expelled from college and came close to being deported."

The judge was silent for what seemed an eternity.

"What if your bride consents to your request to have the phrase 'abandon all others' omitted?" he then asked.

I looked at him in shame and gratitude and nodded.

During the next few weeks, I ostentatiously dated other women. Not only did Mary Ann endure it all, but she granted my request. I had secretly hoped, of course, that her answer would be no. Now there was no way out.

Finally, on Christmas Eve of 1966, in the middle of a snowstorm, we were married, with Hans Morgenthau present as best man. As I kissed my bride, my fear subsided. I sensed that this gentle, loving woman, with her gift of music, might be able to heal the sickness of my soul.

Mary Ann revealed herself to be a woman with a loving and intelligent heart. She suggested I remove the nameplate with the title "Dr." from the door of our apartment. "You are a talented and brilliant man," she said, "and you don't have to announce it with a title. Have confidence in yourself."

In the evenings when I would work, she would usually practice for a concert or recital. I would sometimes interrupt my work and listen. There were fleeting moments when I felt less driven and instead experienced a sense of tranquility and peace.

Hans Morgenthau became a frequent visitor over the following months. I admired the aging scholar not only for his commitment to his work but also for his courageous opposition to the Vietnam War. He had warned against the dangers of the war earlier than many others and had become the subject of fierce official attacks. It had taken me several years to find the courage to address him by his first name. Gradually, however, I lost my initial shyness and soon the dinner table was not quite complete without his presence.

"Have you heard the story about the sexton in the temple?" Hans asked over dessert one night.

"No," I lied. I had heard it twice before.

"On Yom Kippur," Hans began, "the rabbi falls to the ground, beats his chest, and shouts, 'I am nothing.' The cantor, too, falls to the ground, beats his chest, and shouts, 'I am nothing.' Suddenly, the little sexton drops to the floor, shouting, 'I am nothing.' The rabbi looks at the sexton in consternation. 'Look who says he is nothing,' he whispers to the cantor."

On another occasion, when I praised a not particularly brilliant colleague for his modesty, Morgenthau looked at me skeptically. "He has much to be modest about," he quipped laconically.

Several weeks after my marriage, I received a letter from the State Department. A recruitment officer informed me that a high post in the United Nations Secretariat had opened up and he urged me to apply. Somewhat overwhelmed, I hesitated, but Mary Ann reminded me that the United Nations was something I believed in. So, bolstered by her encouragement, I asked for an appointment with U Thant, the secretary-general.

"You would supervise about thirty men and women," said U Thant when we finally met, "and you would be responsible for the preparation of position papers and political analyses for me on a weekly basis." His kind face broke into a smile. "I have read your latest book on the United Nations," he added, "and I would like it very much if you could work for us."

An immense sense of pride washed over me. At last I would be able to enter the world of power and be an adviser to the secretary-general on United Nations policy. I also decided to set up a new institute at City University of New York that would be dedicated to United Nations issues and for which I would raise funds. I thought of Rusty's mother and her prediction that I would make a fortune in America. I determined to give my new assignments everything I had, and so before I wrote my letter of acceptance, I closed my brokerage accounts without a moment of regret. I now had better things to do.

I was given a spacious office in the United Nations Headquarters overlooking the East River and assigned a highly qualified Indian secretary. My immediate supervisor was a Soviet undersecretary. He warned me that any paper prepared by my division would have to be shown to him before it was transmitted to the secretary-general. "Soviet-American balance," he explained, showing his steel-capped teeth in a large smile.

The officers assigned to me, each of which had a separate office and access to a secretary, impressed me greatly. The thirty men and women came from many different countries, most of them having either earned higher academic degrees or gained experience in diplomatic posts throughout the world. I found that they responded well to my enthusiasm and they quickly began to submit excellent political analyses on a variety of subjects. I would spend long hours in discussion with the members of my staff. Then I would take each paper to the Soviet undersecretary and we would bargain, often fiercely, over every page until, finally, the product of these extensive labors was sent up to the secretary-general. U Thant had his suite three floors above my office, but he might as well have been in a different country. I saw him only rarely after that initial interview, usually at diplomatic receptions where he stood patiently in line, shaking a thousand hands with a benign, though somewhat frozen, smile.

Once, after a particularly sharp debate with the Soviet under-secretary over a paper that I considered to be of great importance, I decided to see U Thant. I wanted to clarify my position orally. A secretary ushered me in almost immediately.

"Well, Professor, how is school?" asked U Thant, holding out his hand.

"School is fine, Mr. Secretary-General," I replied, somewhat taken aback, "but may I speak to you about a paper?"

"Oh, yes of course," U Thant replied absentmindedly. "How are you getting along?"

"Fine," I answered. "Have you found my paper helpful?"

"I have been terribly busy lately," U Thant said apologetically. "I really haven't had time to get to them. But your work is very useful," he added quickly after looking at my face.

"Have you seen the recent one we did on the Middle East?" I asked, my heart sinking.

"No, not yet. But do keep up the good work," he repeated, rising from his chair. He held out his hand to me. I looked into his kind and gentle face and was unable to feel any anger. I took his hand.

"Thank you, Mr. Secretary-General," I said, and walked toward the door.

"Professor," I heard U Thant say. I turned around. "In this house," U Thant said quietly, "you must be a philosopher."

I walked down the back stairs to my office. I did not wish to take the elevator since I was not certain I could hold back the tears of frustration that were welling up inside me. For two years, I had supervised and written countless papers for an audience of one, and now I had discovered that there was no audience at all. The papers had been sent into a void and were gathering dust in some remote filing cabinet. I thought of my staff of dedicated officers. Their talent was completely wasted, their hard work useless, their salaries paid for nothing. As for myself, my impact had been zero.

The shock to my ego was so overwhelming that I sat down in the middle of the staircase. It occurred to me that this was how the land surveyor in Franz Kafka's *Castle* must have felt. The hero of the Kafka novel died in the process of trying to reach the owner of the castle, by whom he was supposed to be employed—the bureaucratic obstacles that were placed in his path were too much for him. *Kafka could learn many lessons here,* I thought bitterly, as I got up from the stairs.

I found one of my subordinates waiting for me when I reentered my office. He was a Turk of fierce loyalty and dedication who approached his work with the utmost seriousness. We had already had a dozen conferences about some changes on a paper he had written.

"Last night I thought about what you said, and I have another compromise proposal," Ahmed said.

"Let me see it, Ahmed," I said, my emotions now under control. Over the half hour that we spoke, I noticed his earnest face become flushed and beads of perspiration form on his forehead. But when we had finished discussing his proposal, I saw a smile of satisfaction drawn across his face.

"Thank you, Ahmed," I said to him at the door. "Thank you for your excellent work. The secretary-general will appreciate it."

Then I went to the men's room, locked myself in, and cried.

I remembered the fierce joy I had felt on my first day of work at the United Nations Secretariat. I had believed I would at last be part of a larger integrating cause: that of building a better world order. But now I saw that the reality was men and women, of often high ideals, confined in a world of glass and steel, doomed to labor in deepening frustration and becoming more and more disconsolate. It seemed that we would all finally succumb to the pension system and a relentless mediocrity. There were exceptions to this rule, of course, but the United Nations was still just a mirror of the world's ills. And even though it made little sense to spend one's energies raging at the mirror, I understood that day that I wouldn't live to see the UN Charter's ideals actualized.

CHAPTER 8

1970–1975

In 1970, I was invited by Grinnell College to receive an honorary degree and to give the commencement address. I wondered whether the new president knew about the circumstances of my disappearance from the campus twenty years earlier. A great deal had changed at Grinnell since then, and Dr. Stevens had been dead ten years. Two days before commencement day, however, I received a call.

"We have a revolution here on campus," Grinnell's new president said apologetically. "It's about Cambodia, and there will be no commencement this year."

"Really?" I asked, not quite knowing what to say.

"We will mail you your degree," the president added. "I am truly sorry."

He sounded quite sincere and either did not know about my past or had written off the 1950 episode as belonging to another era. Two weeks later, my honorary doctorate arrived by registered mail, exactly like the undergraduate diploma twenty years before.

Life had settled down once more to a routine. I taught my classes, supervised papers that no one read, and tried to raise money for my anemic institute. I had even begun to work on a new book in my air-conditioned office. No one seemed to mind.

One day, U Thant summoned me to his office.

"Professor," he said quietly, "how would you like to help me end the Vietnam War?"

"I would love to," I blurted out. I told him that I strongly agreed with Hans Morgenthau's position that the war was unwinnable for the United States.

U Thant nodded. "I would like you to ask President Lyndon Johnson and President Ho Chi Minh to come to my hometown of Rangoon, Burma, and negotiate a peace agreement."

My enthusiasm for the UN was instantly reignited. "How?" I wanted to know.

"Ask them to stop the fighting and the dying and turn over the problem to the United Nations," the secretary-general said simply. "And keep this to yourself," he quickly added with a smile.

For the next two years, I worked hard to get the two war leaders to come to Rangoon. Several times, I secured their agreement, but invariably, as the meeting date approached, one of them would cancel. Ho Chi Minh would do so without explanation, but Johnson would declare publicly that he did not wish to be the first American president to lose a war. When U Thant's term expired in 1971, nothing had been accomplished. He died not long thereafter of cancer, or perhaps of grief. I resigned from the United Nations in 1974, and the following year the North Vietnamese overran Saigon and renamed it Ho Chi Minh City.

At the war's end, fifty-eight thousand Americans and three million Vietnamese had died. Some of my students were among the

My parents, Karl and Irene, shortly after they were married in Vienna in 1924

Mutti and me, about 2 years old.

Me as a schoolboy, about 7 years old.

Me in the Viennese Stadtpark sandbox.

Going to America! Oskar and my mother saying goodbye to me at the USS *General Gordon*, Shanghai.

Saying goodbye to Rusty.

My Harvard PhD commencement, 1952.

Eva and I visiting Radcliffe, the "Harvard College" for women, from which Eva graduated.

My mother in San Antonio
at age 87. Photo provided by
Janis Lasser.

The Viennese Stadtpark sandbox
where I played as a child until the
Nazis barred us from all parks.
Photo provided by Janis Lasser.

The last school I attended before
the Hitler Youth ejected me.

My last home in Vienna, 35
Reisnerstrasse.

Receiving an Honorary Doctorate
in Geneva, Switzerland.

In Edi's office in Vienna, 1990.
Photo provided by Janis Lasser.

Dr. Ryoichi Manabe, Janis Lasser, and me at our first reunion in Tokyo.

Uncle Edi and me at the kaffeehaus.
Photo provided by Janis Lasser.

First year in Texas with Janis.

With Janis at Tavern on the Green in NYC.

Eva and me, taking a walk through
Harvard's campus.

Rusty Wunder and me
arm-in-arm again.

New York, 1978. Photo provided by Janis Lasser.

Eva and me in San Francisco, having just visited
the Golden Gate Bridge.

Eve, Michael, and Rusty Wunder in
Kenthurst, Australia. Photo provided
by Janis Lasser.

Rusty and his granddaughter, Ellen,
summer of 2011.

Young at heart, walking with Rusty in Bedford, New York, 2005.

Rusty Wunder and me.

fallen. Consumed by grief and guilt, I began to work on a new book, *Why Nations Go to War*.

One day, on a speaking tour of Florida, I visited an acquaintance in Miami.

"I am expecting an overseas call from a business associate in London," said Colonel Flynn. "She has a question about the United Nations; could you talk to her?"

"Why not?" I responded.

"Her name is Laura Larrabee," Flynn said. "She is an international financier."

Shortly afterward, the call came through and I picked up the phone.

"I hear you work for the United Nations," said a warm and friendly voice. "Would you make an inquiry for me at the Mexican mission?"

"Sure," I replied. I liked the way the woman laughed on the telephone; she made me want to laugh with her.

Two weeks later, the phone rang in my office. It was Laura Larrabee calling for the information she had asked for.

"I would very much like to meet you," Laura said after a brief pause in our conversation.

"I am arriving at Kennedy Airport the day after tomorrow," she continued. "Could you meet me there?"

I hesitated. Going out to Kennedy would kill an entire afternoon.

I was mildly annoyed the day Laura was to arrive. The London flight was almost an hour late and the traffic to the airport had been heavy. I didn't quite know why I was meeting this strange woman from London, but I was curious. Besides, she had a charming laugh, so maybe she would cheer me up. I peered through the glass partition into the area where passengers were beginning to push their luggage carts. Thirty minutes passed, and I started to get angry. Suddenly the doors slid open and I stared in utter disbelief at a blond woman. She had the face of a chubbier Lisl, whom I hadn't seen in more than thirty years.

Laura had expressed a desire to see the United Nations on the night of her arrival from London. She had never had the time to see it, she explained, and asked that I give her a guided tour. As I led her through the Security Council chamber, she explained to me how she had worked for an RCA executive but had gotten bored after a ten-year stint and had decided to become a financier. She then served as middleman, or broker, between banks and governments, negotiating large international loans. At present, she was working on behalf of the Austrian and Greek governments, which were interested in borrowing large sums of money.

"Would you like to attend one of my institute seminars tomorrow evening at the university?" I asked, rather flattered. A distinguished colleague from the United Nations was scheduled to speak at dinner and I was eager to make an impression on this important lady financier.

Laura did not call the following day, and I assumed that I probably would not see her again. As I walked the few blocks from the United Nations to the university, I found myself wishing that she had called. To my pleasant surprise, on entering the dining room, I saw her blond hair at the far end of the bar. She was holding a glass of orange juice and talking to a colleague.

"Hi," she waved at me. "I have just been telling your friend that neither one of us likes alcohol."

"Come and sit at the head table," I said, genuinely delighted.

I was eager to demonstrate my gifts as a lecturer to my guest, but I was annoyed to discover that I was not the main speaker. As it turned out, however, the guest lecturer was stimulating and Laura joined freely in the discussion after dinner. She did so intelligently and with a sense of humor.

"It seems to me that the UN is a pretty poor credit risk," she had said to me with a laugh after the meeting. "But you certainly are running a marvelous institute. Thank you for inviting me."

On the way to her hotel, I had told Laura about my problems with the institute.

"I think I can help you," she said without hesitation. "I know some businesspeople in Europe whom I will ask to make contributions. And if my deal in Vienna goes through," she added after a short pause, "I will set aside a part of my own commissions. I am a businesswoman, but I have a deep commitment to world peace."

Her generosity touched me. It seemed genuine and spontaneous.

We had lunch in the delegates' dining room at the UN.

"I have to fly to Vienna soon on business," Laura said. "Do you know anyone there? I don't even speak the language."

"I have an uncle in Vienna," I said. "He is my one surviving relative from the Nazi Holocaust. I will write him and ask that he show you Vienna."

"You will have to call him," Laura said, and laughed. "I am supposed to be in Vienna the day after tomorrow. But why don't you come up and write down his address for me?"

Laura occupied a luxurious suite on the top floor of the hotel where she was staying. When we reached her door, she took off her mink coat and threw it on one of the two double beds before taking out her black diary and handing it to me.

"There is room on the last page," she said, passing me a silver pencil.

I sat down at the little hotel desk and jotted down my uncle's name and address. Then I rose and handed the diary and pencil back to her. She took both, but did not let go of my hands. Without an instant's hesitation, she pulled me toward her and kissed me.

"I am married, Laura," I managed to stammer, catching my breath.

"I know," Laura murmured. "You told me that you are happily married. I won't make any demands of you; I am hardly ever in the United States. I am a proud woman and it is not easy for me to say this, but I want you to make love to me tonight."

It was past midnight and I was concerned about Mary Ann. I did not want to call her from Laura's suite and I suddenly felt a flood of guilt.

"Laura," I said, "I have to go home."

"I know," she responded, without a trace of anger. "I will call you from Vienna, for a letter of recommendation, a character reference. It will help me in your hometown."

"I'll be happy to, Laura," I said. I felt stiff and formal next to this uninhibited creature. "I'll call my uncle right away; it's already morning in Europe."

"Don't come to the airport tomorrow. I hate good-byes. But I want you to be there when I get back, whenever that will be."

"Have a good trip," I said. The phrase struck me as hollow and a little stupid.

Needing time to think, I walked several blocks before I hailed a cab.

Mary Ann had been waiting up for me. "So how was the lady financier?"

"Fine," I replied.

"I heard she is fat and rich. Is that true?"

"That's right," I said as I went to the telephone. "Give me Vienna," I said to the operator.

I hadn't seen my uncle Edi for more than thirty years. He had immigrated to Australia after the Nazis occupied Vienna and then settled in New Zealand. He had prospered there after the war but was finally so overwhelmed by homesickness for his favorite Viennese *kaffeehaus*, the Café Prückel on Stubenring, that, at the age of seventy, he decided to return. A story made the rounds that when he appeared there, the old headwaiter took one look and immediately, without a word, brought Edi his favorite breakfast: two freshly baked buttered rolls, a soft-boiled egg, and coffee with whipped cream. After an absence of almost three decades, Edi found this tactful matter-of-fact behavior more touching than the most effusive welcome.

I had not returned to Vienna since the war. There had been no reason for me to do so, nor did I wish to stir up memories. I was acutely aware, however, as I waited on the telephone, that I should have made the effort to contact my dead father's brother earlier. In my heart, I knew that I had not done so for fear of what I might find out about my father.

"Hello," said a voice at the other end.

"Uncle Edi, this is your nephew, Hans." A strange feeling went through me as I used my childhood name.

"Hans. My God," said the voice on the other side of the Atlantic. "How I would love to see you. Are you coming to Vienna?"

I suddenly realized that Uncle Edi obviously thought that I was calling to tell him I was passing through Vienna.

"Yes," I said without thinking, "I will visit you this summer." Then I quickly told him about Laura. Edi promised to be helpful.

"Be sure to come," he insisted. "I want to see you once more in this life."

"Yes, Uncle Edi, of course I will," I heard myself say.

After I hung up, I began to cry. Mary Ann's hand softly touched my shoulder, her gentle face expressing concern.

"I don't know what the hell I am getting into," I said, trying to stop my tears. "How would you like to visit Vienna this summer?"

Five days later, I received an overseas call at my office.

"Happy New Year." It was Laura, her voice clear and warm. "Your uncle is a lovely man; he has been showing me Vienna. I have a surprise for you!" She laughed and put Edi on the line.

"You have sent a charming emissary," said Uncle Edi. "When will I see you?"

"This summer," I said quickly, suddenly finding myself looking forward to seeing the old man.

"We are at the bank," Laura chimed in after getting on an extension. "Things are going very well. Can you send me that letter?"

"Sure, Laurie," I answered. "What shall I say?"

"Well, say that I have an impeccable reputation and that I have closed numerous financial transactions to the satisfaction of both borrower and lender."

"Fine, Laurie," I said as I copied down the phrase.

Laura called me periodically during the next few weeks. I found myself looking forward to these calls from Vienna, London, or Geneva. On one occasion, she told me that she loved my book. It deserved the widest readership, she said, and she would do her best to get it translated into as many languages as possible. I felt a sudden rush of gratitude. My book had not exactly been a commercial success and was now destined to become a paperback for the college market. Laura seemed to recognize that academic recognition was no longer satisfying to me. What my ego craved was a quantum leap into literary fame.

The phone rang again one bleak afternoon in February. It was Laura, calling from Geneva.

"I am coming through New York tomorrow," she said. "Can you meet me at Kennedy?"

"How long can you stay?" I asked.

"I am changing planes for Mexico, so about eight hours."

The next day Laura and I were sitting in the lounge waiting for her plane.

"I have a surprise for you," she said. "I have spoken to Bobby Sarnoff and suggested to him that RCA distribute your book as a Christmas gift to all its employees and its best customers." *She calls him Bobby?* I said to myself, and wondered how she knew him so well. *She certainly must be legitimate,* I naively thought.

"How is that possible?" I asked, delighted.

"It's logical," Laura said. "Your book is published by Random House, and Random House is owned by RCA. RCA is committed to the improvement of communications throughout the world, and your book talks about the new openings to Russia and China."

I looked at Laura. Her logic made sense, or so I thought.

"How many copies would that mean?" I asked.

"About four hundred thousand."

One night, I was watching the evening news—the president and Henry Kissinger were briefing reporters after their return from China—and I swelled with gratitude for Laura. I knew that soon my book would have its day, too. Besides, Laura had told me before she left for Mexico that her Austrian transaction would close soon. A second one, in Greece, she said, was also going well. I had given her another letter. Thanks to Laura, my gloom had lifted. I would finally become a well-known author and would be able to finance my pet project at the university.

I couldn't help thinking of her often; she was a sensual, attractive woman. And I knew there should be no complications with my marriage, since our occasional trysts would not be difficult to hide. I would have both adventure and security, and might even have a crack at literary glory.

After she left for Mexico, Laura would call about once or twice a week. At times, she would call me at home in the middle of the night. "A call for you from Tehran, Iran," the operator would say. Groggy with sleep, I would stagger to my study and pick up the telephone. I did not want Mary Ann to overhear the conversation.

"So where is she now?" Mary Ann asked when I came back to bed.

"Tehran," I replied.

"My God, maybe she's a spy."

I desperately hoped Mary Ann didn't suspect anything.

In April, one of these nocturnal calls came in from Rome.

"I have asked for an audience with the Holy Father. I would like to give him a copy of your book."

"Thank you, Laurie," I said, half asleep. "That's wonderful."

"The book project is going well at RCA," Laura continued.

"Thank you, Laurie," I repeated, not quite knowing what to say. There was a brief pause at the other end.

"I will spend Easter weekend in Rome. Do you think you could join me here?"

I hesitated, suddenly fully awake, my mind racing. I desperately wanted to say yes, but did not wish to hurt Mary Ann. Confronted with the classic married man's dilemma, my marriage's banality and my own cowardice repelled me.

"Of course I'll come, Laurie," I heard myself say.

"And bring some more books, I've run out. And some stationery. I may need a few more letters."

I told Mary Ann of my decision the next morning at breakfast. "Laura wants me to come to Rome," I said. "She is placing a large order of my book with RCA."

Mary Ann looked at me quizzically. "RCA is in New York, why do you have to go to Rome?"

"She is helping me finance the UN institute," I said, "and she needs me there on business."

"What do you know about her business?" Mary Ann persisted.

I felt my anger rising. Mary Ann's questions were both innocent and logical.

"She wants me to meet a Vatican official," I said, "who is interested in my book."

It was a stupid lie that had occurred to me instinctively, without reflection. Mary Ann looked at me with her gentle eyes. I saw the hurt in them and realized that she knew the truth. A sinking feeling came over me. But I had made a commitment and was no longer able to turn back. Mary Ann lapsed into a heavy silence. I was grateful that she didn't make a scene. But even if she had begged me on her knees, I suddenly realized with horror that I would still board the plane to Rome.

Even though my guilt was great, the temptation to go was even greater. A pretty woman who reminded me of my boyhood love, and who had promised to make my dreams come true and make me rich and famous, had invited me for a holiday in Rome. For six years, I rationalized, I had been a loving husband to my wife. Surely, I was entitled to a weekend of adventure after years of discipline and work.

"When will you come back?" Mary Ann asked, reaching for my hand.

"In three days, maybe four," I said, packing a small valise and avoiding my wife's eyes. Then, fighting my guilty conscience, I left the house and jumped into a cab.

Laura was waiting for me at the airport. In the cab, on the way to the hotel, she showed me a letter. It was from the secretary of state of the Vatican. In it, the official thanked her for having transmitted a copy of my book to the Holy Father.

"The Pope gave me an audience," Laura added. "I told him how much I believed in your work and he gave me his blessing."

I believed her. I was glad I had come to Rome.

We were sitting in a small café on the Via Veneto. It was a warm spring afternoon and the avenue was crowded with strollers taking in the sun. Laura took my hand and looked at me.

"I have good news for you," she said. "Bobby Sarnoff has approved the book project; the capital appropriations board of RCA has set aside the funds, they want to make it a gift for Christmas."

I was dumbfounded. "What do you think of this?" she asked. She had placed a print of Albrecht Dürer's etching *Praying Hands* on the little coffee table. "We want to place this in every copy of the book with a Christmas message from the president of RCA. Could you draft one or two paragraphs for him?" she asked, her eyes laughing. "After all, you are the author."

Overcome, I nodded in agreement.

"Tomorrow night I fly to Athens," Laura added. "I hope to close a large loan there with the Bank of Greece. If I succeed, I will set aside half a million dollars for your UN institute."

I felt the tears well up within me. "Laurie, I don't know what to say, it's all too much for me to grasp."

"I love you," said Laura. Suddenly, her face had become serious. "And I want to make you happy."

"I have a small token for you, too, Laurie," I said, taking a little box out of my pocket. Before I had left New York, I had gone to a jeweler and bought Laura a string of pearls. I placed the necklace around Laura's neck and kissed her.

"I love you," she repeated. Then, hand in hand, we walked down the Via Veneto.

"I am a little afraid of going to Greece," said Laura. "They have a police state there. I think you'd better give me a letter of protection."

"Of course I will, Laurie. I wish I could go with you. What do you want me to say?"

"Can you say that I work for you?" Laura asked.

I thought for a moment. "I can appoint you as an intern without salary to my peace research unit at the UN institute," I said. It was a practice I had followed with some of my better graduate students. "And I can put you on the board of the institute at the university since you will raise some funds."

"That's great," said Laura. "Then, if I get in trouble with the junta, you won't have to rescue me." She typed the letters and I put my name to them. My ego continued to allow her to manipulate me.

"A call for you from Athens," said the overseas operator. It was a sunny afternoon in May and I was sitting in my office editing a paper.

I heard Laura's voice after I accepted the call. She sounded a bit impatient.

"I have mixed blessings to report," she said. "The governor of the Bank of Greece just had a heart attack; he is seventy-eight years old. We had to postpone the closing and I'll have to come back to Athens. And the Austrians are being difficult, too."

"But there is some good news, too," Laura said, her voice brightening. "I am flying to New York tomorrow and you and I will see the president of RCA. Did you compose the Christmas message for the book?"

"It's been waiting for you on my desk for the last six weeks," I answered happily.

Not unexpectedly, relations between Mary Ann and me had become strained since my return from Europe. This was the first time that dissonance was jarring our marriage and, while I loved my wife, I was simply unwilling to give up my mistress. I hoped that by maneuvering adroitly I would be able to hold on to both.

I had bought a new suit ahead of the meeting with the president of RCA. We were to discuss the Christmas message for my book and sign an agreement for my royalties. I was in a fever of anticipation. At one dollar per copy, my royalties would come to four hundred thousand dollars. At eleven o'clock, the phone rang.

"Bobby had to cancel," Laura said. "There was an unexpected crisis. Why don't you and I have lunch together at the UN? And I need more letters. Your secretary can type them while I wait."

"Laurie," I said hesitantly, "four hundred thousand copies is a gigantic order. I shall tell my editor at Random House about it so that he can get them ready."

"Good idea," Laura replied. "The books should be shipped by November. By the way," she continued, "why don't you just write me a couple of 'To Whom It May Concern' letters? Then I don't have to bother you every time I need a letter."

"Sure," I replied, never stopping to examine what was really going on here.

In the afternoon, I saw my editor at Random House. Barry rubbed his forehead thoughtfully.

"We can do it by November," he said after a pause. "It's a fantastic opportunity."

"Once in a lifetime," I agreed.

"We have the plates; all we have to do is print 'em," Barry said. "So just give us the go-ahead."

"In a day or two, I hope," I said.

It was eleven o'clock the following morning and I was wearing my new suit again.

"Bobby's done it again," said Laura, "but he says tomorrow without fail."

I swallowed the anger I felt rising in me. After all, I supposed, it wasn't Laura's fault that the chief executive of RCA had more important things to do than meet with a middle-aged author.

"But now that we have a couple of hours to spare, you can do me a small favor. You can open a special bank account, giving me power of attorney. It's just a matter of convenience; you could pay some petty bills for me while I am gone; I will make the deposits."

"I suppose so," I replied. I was completely blind as to where this would lead.

We went to my bank and I asked to see the manager.

"There is no problem," said the bank official. "The lady will make the deposits, but you, Professor, will receive the monthly statements."

"That's fine with me," I said to Laura. "I'll save the monthly statements for you."

"While we are here," said Laura, "why don't you open a safe-deposit box? I'd like to put some of my valuables in it."

I looked at Laura with surprise.

"I fly a great deal," Laura explained, "and I carry too many documents around with me."

We went to the rear of the bank and a clerk filled out the necessary forms. Laura placed some papers in the box and I received the key.

"If one of these days my plane should crash, you are the executor of my will," Laura said to me in a serious tone. "You are the only person in the world whom I really trust."

The following day, I sat in my office, unable to work. Mary Ann had made a scene the night before and the guilt was strangling me. I was not in love with Laura, yet I was hurting my wife desperately because Laura had become my key to fame and power. If I could only learn to walk the tightrope, I thought, I would be able to still that hunger that had been eating at my guts. Suddenly, it occurred to me that I was behaving like a whore. Worse than a whore, I thought, because whores had no one to come home to while I had a wife whose love and trust I was using as a crutch for my adventures. What if Mary Ann left me? Would I exchange her for a life with Laura?

The telephone interrupted my train of thought.

"I am afraid to tell you this," said Laura, "but Bobby suddenly had to leave town."

"To hell with Bobby," I screamed into the telephone, "and to hell with your damn promises!" I was hardly able to control my rage. "I suppose he will see us tomorrow," I said sarcastically in a calmer tone.

"No," said Laura, "I have to leave the day after tomorrow. We'll have to meet with him when I get back." Wracked by guilt toward both my wife and mistress, I slumped down in my chair.

"So how was RCA?" said Mary Ann when I sat down at dinner. "Did she make you into a great author yet?"

I didn't answer. I was too sick with guilt and rage.

"I wouldn't count your royalties yet, if I were you," she said wisely.

When next I met Laura, she rebuked me for being angry with her the last time we spoke. I stupidly felt guilty and apologized to her. I sheepishly tried to make it up to her and gave her the Christmas message I had drafted for her to take to Bob Sarnoff. She folded it up without reading it. She was controlling me and I was reacting like a scared little boy.

"Well, what do you say now?" I asked Mary Ann later as I showed her the Christmas message for my book. My need to prove to her that I was on my way to literary stardom had made me tactless. Besides, Mary Ann had sulked around the house for weeks and the icy atmosphere was unbearable.

"We can get you a concert grand now," I said, trying to bribe her into a smile. Mary Ann made no response.

"How about a trip to Europe?" I asked. "I would love to show you Vienna." Mary Ann's face lit up.

We were planning to spend two weeks in Vienna on our way to Russia, where the Soviet government had invited me to give some lectures at Moscow University during the summer. I wished to keep my promise to visit Uncle Edi and also wanted to patch up my relationship with Mary Ann. I had told Laura about my Russian lecture tour before she left for Europe, but I had not said anything about visiting Vienna.

A portly man with a balding head came toward us at the gate.

"Hans," he said, his eyes moist with tears, "you look exactly like your father. Even without the picture I would have recognized you right away." The small man hugged me to him as if I were his son.

"Uncle Edi," I said, a bit embarrassed, "this is my wife Mary Ann."

"Enchanted," said Edi in a courtly manner that seemed completely natural, and he kissed Mary Ann's hand.

We drove into town in Uncle Edi's Volkswagen. Vienna hadn't changed too much, I thought, as we approached the Ringstrasse.

The next few days, Edi drove us all over Vienna. He was affectionate and often placed his hand around my shoulder in a warm and spontaneous gesture. To Mary Ann, he was considerate and solicitous. His wife never came along; Edi mentioned that she had not been well lately and didn't care to elaborate. Despite his genuine warmth and an infectious sense of humor, I sensed a profound sadness about him.

"I think you should talk to him," Mary Ann said to me after one of our drives into Vienna's surrounding woods. "I think he wants to be alone with you, and we won't be here much longer."

So Edi and I took some time and went to the Café Prückel *kaffeehaus*. It was ten o'clock on a weekday morning and the place was almost empty. The headwaiter had just brought our breakfast on a silver tray and had withdrawn silently with a respectful bow. Edi was stirring his coffee.

"Your father and I used to come here more than forty years ago," he said suddenly. "You know, I loved your father very much."

"Edi," I said, mustering up all my courage, "how did it happen? Was it because of the Nazis?"

Edi kept stirring his coffee. "It was in 1933, the year Hitler came to power," he replied. "Karl—I mean your father—was heavily in debt. The creditors were beating down his door, and in his despair, he did something stupid: he gave one of his creditors a large check." Edi cleared his throat and hesitated before going on. "Anyway, the check bounced because there was no money in the account and he was arrested for fraud."

"My God," I said, "couldn't he have borrowed the money from someone?"

"He tried, but no one would lend it to him," Edi said. "So he went to jail." He stirred his coffee again. I noticed that the cup was almost empty. "And there was something else," Edi said with a sigh. "Your father had an affair with another woman. Your mother found out about it and became hysterical."

"What do you mean?" I asked. "Did she leave him?"

"Yes," Edi answered. "An unfaithful husband who was in jail was too much for her. She told him that she would leave him and take you with her."

I felt a black rage welling up inside me.

"When he got out of jail, after a few months," Edi continued, "your mother wouldn't take him back."

"And his lady friend?" I asked. I was too embarrassed to refer to the woman as my father's mistress.

"She had disappeared," Edi replied.

"And so he was alone?" I asked.

"That's right," Edi nodded sadly. "And then, he went to Palestine, and there, in a moment of despair, he did it."

"How?" I asked, in shock from the details I had already learned.

"He swallowed poison," Edi said, and looked at me. I noticed that his eyes had filled with tears. Shaking, I reached for my uncle's hand. "He loved your mother," Edi sobbed. "He missed your mother and he missed you."

I held my uncle's hand for a very long time, not knowing whether I was comforting him or trying to draw strength from him. A surge of hopeless love for this old man swept over me.

"Would you like to visit him?" Edi's eyes searched mine.

I looked at him questioningly.

"I brought his remains back from Israel; the cemetery is not too far from here. I've been there twice already since I've come back."

We rose from the table and left the small café. Edi took the highway that led out of the city.

"He is not in the municipal cemetery," he said. The explanation sounded more like an apology.

Soon we were in the suburbs and I no longer recognized the streets. Edi turned into a narrow country road and stopped at the entrance of a tiny cemetery. We walked through the gate and I saw hundreds of little gray stones with names and dates in no particular order. Edi had begun to walk faster, his eyes fixed on the ground.

"He is all the way at the end," he said apologetically. We walked to the back fence of the cemetery and there, bunched closely together in the corner, were about a dozen little stones. They were clearly separated from the rest by a low fence, almost like pariahs.

"Why is he here like this?" I asked Edi. I knew the answer, but for some reason I had to ask anyway.

"This is the plot for suicides. They are not allowed to be buried in sanctified ground."

I looked at the little marker that bore my father's name and the year 1934. My mind was racing, but my heart felt numb; it was as though a part of me had split off. I forced myself to look once more at the little stone. How strange, I thought, that the corpse that had been buried here almost forty years ago had made me what I was. He was still able to reach out and affect my life after there was literally nothing left of him. It seemed insane.

"How long do skulls last in the ground?" I asked Edi.

My uncle looked at me with surprise, and I looked away, ashamed of my tactless question. Edi drove back in silence after that.

"At least we know where he is buried," he said finally. "More than we can say about six million other Jews who were murdered by the Nazis."

"Or about Mozart," I added in a lame attempt at humor.

"Your Laura is a good businesswoman and I think she is in love with you," Edi said suddenly, without transition. "But you should be careful," he added thoughtfully, "you have a beautiful and loving wife."

Embarrassed and taken by surprise, I sank back in my seat.

"I speak from experience," Edi said. "I couldn't give up women either and finally Lola had enough." Edi turned onto the highway leading back into the city. "We are like two strangers now, living in the same house."

"Seems to run in the family," I answered.

"What do you mean?" Edi asked.

"Women," I replied.

Edi broke into a sudden laugh. Gratefully, he touched my arm, my answer apparently releasing the tension. Soon we were back in the inner city.

"I am glad I came, Uncle Edi," I managed to say haltingly. "But in two days, we are off to Russia."

"Please come through Vienna on your way back to New York," Edi said, his voice almost pleading.

Mary Ann and I stopped in Prague on our way to Russia, where a pervasive grayness hovered over the old city. We looked down on the Moldau River from one of Prague's majestic bridges. I was overcome by sadness. Charles Jordan, who had helped me to America and who had been so concerned about how we children survived, had been murdered in Prague five years earlier; his body had been found floating in the Moldau. He had been helping Jews escape from Czechoslovakia to Israel. Rumor had it that the Soviet secret police had collaborated with Palestinian Arabs in his murder, but it was difficult to prove.

After a day's stay, we left Prague. I felt too unhappy in the city I had once loved so much.

The next day, we arrived in Moscow. Intourist put us up in a cavernous hotel near Red Square. While I was lecturing, Mary Ann was inspecting music schools, and at night we fell into bed, totally exhausted. One evening we were unable to find our room and a bellhop had to help us.

"Largest hotel in the world," he said proudly, pocketing a tip.

The night before we left, just before dawn, the phone rang.

"Who could be calling us at this hour?" Mary Ann asked sleepily.

"I am calling from Zurich," said Laura. "It took me a few days to track you down."

I broke into a sweat.

"That's nice," I whispered into the receiver.

"I know you can't talk," said Laura, "but I just wanted to tell you that I plan to be in New York in about a week."

"That's nice," I repeated, sweating.

"I have good news about the book project and the institute," Laura said happily.

Lying into the phone, I said, "I am looking forward to the lecture."

"Who was it?" Mary Ann asked.

"The secret police," I answered, in a nocturnal attempt at humor.

I was drenched in perspiration. Trembling, I crept back into bed and cuddled up to Mary Ann. She did not move away. Soon I fell asleep and dreamt about Edi. There was something strange about him. He was looking at me imploringly and trying to tell me something. Yet, no matter how hard I tried, I couldn't understand. He seemed to be speaking in a language I had never heard before. I woke up suddenly, badly frightened. The dream had had a nightmare quality. Then with a flash of terror I remembered: in the dream, Edi had looked at me with the face of my dead father.

It had been almost four months since I had seen Laura. She had called from Geneva a few days after Mary Ann and I returned from Russia and announced that she would be delayed. "Those damn closings," she had said. "There is always some last-minute hitch." She then asked for several more letters, which I mailed to Zurich and Geneva. With each call and each letter she asked me to write for her, my anxiety increased since she failed to mention the book project or any contributions to the institute. My editor at Random House had telephoned me twice already to inquire whether he could go ahead. I told him that there had been a delay.

I had also told colleagues at the university that I expected a large funding for the UN institute. There, too, I had to give evasive answers. Not wishing to arouse Laura's anger, I had not mentioned my concern to her in our transatlantic conversations. But now it was October and only a crash schedule could meet a Christmas deadline.

Without daring to admit it to myself, I had practically given up all hope. Laura's announcement that the project had been postponed one again was, therefore, not a shock, but a reprieve.

My life had settled down once more into a routine. I taught my classes and was hard at work on my new book. Occasionally, I telephoned Mr. Hewitt at RCA. He was always courteous though somewhat noncommittal, only ever assuring me that he and Laura were handling the project.

The usual financial worries were irritating me in regard to the institute, although my home life had improved somewhat. As Laura passed through New York less and less often, Mary Ann's anger had subsided. I could not deny, however, that I looked forward to Laura's brief visits with a deep and secret thrill.

"My next trip will be a long one," Laura said to me on her next call. "I think it might be as long as half a year. I've decided to concentrate on the Middle East and Africa."

Spring and summer came and went and I heard less and less from Laura. She would call occasionally from Africa or from the Middle East, usually to ask for yet another letter. The conversations were perfunctory and brief, and Laura sounded increasingly like a stranger.

Instead of exhilarating me, as in the past, each conversation left me depressed. I went into commodities again in an effort to dispel my deepening malaise. My rationalization was that I could afford to lose money, now that ten times that amount would soon materialize from RCA. On a deeper level, though, the money had become a symbol of my guilt, a nagging feeling that I was using Laura as a vehicle to fame and power. In my self-destructive mood, I did the exact opposite of what my brokers urged. I was advised to buy silver futures and went short; I was told that gold would triple in price and promptly sold some contracts short. To my amazement, I turned out to be right on both these moves and soon tripled my investment.

Both my brokers spoke to me in awe and praised my acumen and courage. The time had obviously come to short the market, they declared. The next candidate, in their opinion, was soybeans. I was urged to go short immediately, as prices were about to fall precipitously. This time I went along and went short a huge amount of beans. Barely had I done so when, as if on some satanic signal, prices began to rise in a steep, almost uninterrupted climb. Four weeks later, after paying up four margin calls, I was almost totally wiped out. But I wasn't even angry when my broker called in his usual sepulchral tone when things went badly. In fact, I was relieved, almost as if justice had been done.

One day in the early fall, the phone rang in my office.

"A call from Brazzaville," the operator said.

"You mean the Congo?" I asked, a little startled.

Of course, it was Laura.

"Are you coming to New York?" I asked, cheered up by her voice. "I might be able to introduce you to the UN ambassador to the Congo."

The Congolese ambassador was a dignified man who, from time to time, attended my seminars at the university. He had studied at the Sorbonne, had absorbed its intellectual atmosphere, and was an ardent defender of the independence of his little country in the heart of Africa. "Rather poor and free," he liked to say, "than rich and living in servitude." When I asked him whether I could introduce an international financier to him, he smiled politely and agreed immediately.

"Bring him to my office whenever you wish," he said.

"It's a lady, Mr. Ambassador," I corrected him.

"All the better," he said diplomatically.

Laura met the ambassador and said, "Mr. Ambassador, your government is trying to borrow one hundred million dollars." The ambassador smiled politely. "I have assembled a consortium of banks that are willing to arrange the loan, but I have to get authorization from your president."

"If the professor here is willing to vouch for you," the ambassador replied after having listened to my translation, "I will give you a visa to my country and a letter to my president. We are a poor country and I know that we have difficulty borrowing money from the big banks." He paused and turned his head in my direction. "But I know that you, Professor, have a warm spot in your heart for the small and poor. A friend of yours is a friend of mine and of my country."

At four o'clock in the afternoon, Laura and I were in a taxi again, on our way to Kennedy Airport with all the documents she needed. I explained to her that the United States doesn't even have diplomatic relations with Congo. I had foolishly given her more reference letters on my UN letterhead stationery. Since this woman had come into my life and dazzled me with promises of fame and fortune, I had stopped thinking clearly. My ego had clouded my judgment every step of the way. The stupidity of writing these letters for her never occurred to me. The staggering troubles that awaited me would shake my world.

Laura looked at me with undisguised contempt. "I am not afraid to go to Africa alone," she said. "I fly all over the world while you sit in your air-conditioned office."

I said nothing. It was true; I had decided not to go with her, but for a different reason. When I had mentioned the possibility to Mary Ann, she had become furious. I was simply not prepared to risk my marriage for a safari into the heart of Africa.

CHAPTER 9

1975

A few days before Christmas, my secretary knocked at the door. "There is someone on the phone who wants urgently to speak with you," she said. I picked up the telephone.

"This is Inspector Kraft of the United States Postal Service," he said harshly.

"Postal Service?" I repeated, confused.

"I would like to see you," said the voice.

"May I ask what this is all about?" I asked politely.

"There is a criminal investigation in progress."

"A criminal investigation?" I repeated mechanically. My entire body had begun to tremble. "About whom?" I asked.

"About Miss Larrabee, and about you," answered the cold, flat voice.

We set a time to meet in my office at the UN the next day. I didn't sleep at all the night before, playing every scenario I could think of in my head. I was dressed by sunrise and waiting for them in my office well before nine o'clock. I told my secretary I was expecting two men and she should send them directly in. I couldn't stop sweating. They were right on time.

"I am Inspector Kraft and this is Inspector Slade." Each handed me a card. The men were nondescript, dressed alike in dark suits and narrow black ties. They looked to be in their thirties.

"What can I do for you, inspectors?" I asked, refusing to be drawn into preliminary pleasantries.

"Do you know Miss Laura Larrabee?" Kraft asked.

"Yes," I replied.

"Did you write this letter for her?" Kraft placed before me a copy of the letter I had written, on Laura's behalf, to the Viennese bank almost two years before.

"She promised to raise money for an academic pet project of mine," I replied.

"How well do you know her?" Slade continued.

"Quite well, I think," I said.

"On what basis did you write this sentence? 'Miss Laura Larrabee has an impeccable reputation and has closed numerous financial transactions to the satisfaction of both borrower and lender.'" Kraft read the passage in a monotone. Those were some of the words Laura had dictated to me to write for her. I never questioned what she had asked me to say. I wrote them all mindlessly.

I had broken out in a sweat. "I know her well," I stammered finally.

"Do you know of any transaction that she actually closed?" Slade asked.

I shook my head.

"Do you know any lender?"

"No," I said.

"Or any borrower?"

Again, I shook my head. "I simply took her word for it," I said. There was a pause.

"Do you have an intimate relationship with her?" asked Kraft.

I nodded again. By now I was so terrified that I was unable to speak. There was another pause as the two men glanced at one another.

"That's all the questions we've got for now," Kraft said as he flipped his small notebook closed and stuffed it into his coat pocket. "We'll be talking to you again, Dr. Stoessinger."

They both shook my hand, but I couldn't make eye contact with either of them. My clammy palm would have given me away if the sweat on my forehead hadn't already betrayed the composure I was trying to feign. As soon as I was sure they were gone, I got on the phone, desperately trying to contact Laura.

"Laura, thank God I reached you," I cried in relief. I had finally tracked Laura down in a hotel in London. "The United States government thinks we are in cahoots to commit fraud," I stammered into the telephone. "I beg you to come back."

There was a pause at the other end.

"If you ever loved me, please come back," I begged, hanging on to the phone as if it were a lifeline.

"Meet me at Kennedy tomorrow night," Laura said after a brief pause.

"Thank you, Laurie," I said, weeping with relief. "I'll be there."

The London flight was half an hour late. I stood at the sliding doors again as the memory of a similar scene two years earlier flashed through my mind. A pilot walked out of the door.

"Was the plane full?" I asked.

"Almost empty," said the pilot. "Not much doing from London this time of year." About a dozen passengers filed past me. Desperately, I searched each face. And suddenly I knew that Laura was not going to get off that plane.

"I missed the flight," Laura said on the telephone, "but I reached Kraft. I told him I was sending a courier with some funds."

"Thank you, Laurie," I said, my despair giving way to renewed hope.

"And I have even added interest," said Laura. "The man is coming with a cashier's check for sixty-four thousand five hundred dollars, made to John Ashley. The courier's name is George Watson. You can meet him tomorrow night at Kennedy."

"Same flight?" I asked.

"Same flight," said Laura.

Later, I called Kraft.

"That's right," Kraft said, "she called me, too." His voice sounded a shade friendlier. "Bring the check in to me as soon as possible."

"Of course I will, inspector," I said eagerly.

This time the plane was half an hour early. Twenty passengers got off. I had George Watson paged, but no one answered to his name. Finally, in desperation, I managed to get a copy of the list of passengers. The name Watson was nowhere to be seen.

"Watson had a personal emergency," Laura said on the phone. "But I am telexing the money bank to bank. I have already phoned Kraft."

"That's right," Kraft said, "she called me again." His voice sounded cold and threatening. "You two better stop cooking up ploys to throw me off the track."

I was trembling again.

"Didn't she send a telex?" I asked desperately.

"She sent a telex promising that, by tomorrow, she would transmit sixty-four thousand five hundred dollars."

"Thank God," I managed to say weakly as I hung up the phone.

The next afternoon, Kraft called. "I have not received the money," he said coldly. "The bank has not received it, either."

"She told me it would be here today," I said with shortness of breath.

"You two seem to think I was born yesterday," Kraft said. There was a cold fury in his voice.

"Believe me, inspector . . ." I began.

"I am turning over the matter to the United States Attorney," Kraft interrupted. "You can expect to be subpoenaed before a grand jury for fraud. I have nothing more to say to you, Doctor." His accent on the title *Doctor* was full of sarcasm.

An hour later, I was shouting at Laura over the phone.

"Laurie," I said desperately. "You didn't send the money and now I will be indicted for fraud. Kraft thinks I am a thief. I will lose my job." In my terror, I had begun to shout. "I beg you to come back, I beg you on my life."

There was silence on the other end.

"Please, Laurie," I pled. "Please come back." I stopped pleading and waited for her answer. I heard nothing. "Laurie," I screamed, "are you there?" Suddenly through the static, I heard her broken voice.

"Yes, I am here," she said, coldly. "I am here," she laughed.

"Laurie!" I shrieked, and dropped the telephone. The receiver fell on top of a glass of water from which I had been drinking. The glass shattered. I reached for the receiver. "Laurie!" I shrieked again. "What are you saying? Why are you laughing?!" My hand was bleeding heavily. I had cut myself on a piece of glass and blood was dripping on my desk.

All I could hear was the cruel laughter. "Yes, I am here," said Laura. "I am here, and I am going to destroy you."

"Why?! Why?!" I yelled. "I don't understand!" But the connection was broken.

The next few months were a special kind of hell. A grand jury indicted me for fraud, believing that I was the thief and Laura was only an accomplice. My attorney advised me that it would be wise to plead guilty to a lesser charge, called misprision, which meant failure to report someone else's crime. As I pondered this possibility, a poem by Rudyard Kipling that I had read long ago in China as a boy suddenly flashed through my mind: "If you can meet with Triumph and Disaster, and treat those two impostors just the same," the English poet had written, "Then you will be a Man, my son." I certainly wasn't acting like a man by the old poet's standards. It was true, I had been manipulated and used and had been the victim of a terrible injustice. I couldn't believe she had victimized me this way. It was also true that I had pled guilty to a crime when in fact I had not committed one. Yet, I knew, too, that I was far from innocent. Gradually the answer came to me. What had brought this to pass was my hunger for the outer trappings, the titles and the merit badges, the pursuit of money, fame, and power.

The books that I had written were to give me value where I felt none. The famous people whom I had pursued were to cover me with bits of their reflected glory. The lectures I had delivered were to reap the adulation of a thousand strangers. And my gambling had been the magic wand that was to protect me from facing my ultimate mortality.

Laura, it gradually dawned upon me, had been a mirror of my life. At the time I met her, I had gone about as far as I could go. Mine had been a career well done but not one that was truly great. Middle age had come and the end was nearer now than the beginning. Limits would pervade my life much more than possibilities. Laura's promises had hit me where I was most vulnerable: the hope that somehow, magically, decline could be arrested and youth's climb resumed. Now this illusion had been shattered, my ordeal having forced me to separate the trapping from the substance, the wasted motion from the inner value. Long ago, I had become someone I was not. If I now decided to go on living, I might finally discover who I was. I would have to start all over. "What happens now?" I asked my attorney, David. "We go before a federal judge and make your plea and then you will be sentenced."

"Sentenced?" I echoed fearfully.

"That's right," said David.

"When must I make this plea?" I asked.

"Tomorrow morning," David said.

The high-ceilinged courthouse chamber resounded with the echoes of many muffled voices. About a hundred people were sitting on rows of benches awaiting their turn. Lawyers in well-pressed suits walked about officiously, briefcases in hand. Suddenly a red-faced bailiff rose.

"Hear ye, hear ye," he shouted. "God bless the United States and this honorable Court."

It was true, I thought, *I had protected Laura.* The thought of reporting her to the authorities had never even occurred to me. After all, we had been lovers. The Via Veneto flashed through my mind. "I want to make you happy," Laura had said. *Perhaps she was a thief,* I thought, *but a thief who had once loved me.*

The red-faced bailiff announced the arrival of the judge and a tall black-robed figure entered. I noticed a few reporters in the gallery. Everyone rose. The scene struck me as both awesome and a bit theatrical. It was as if a play were about to begin and no one but the black-robed figure knew the ending. David rose and spoke briefly and eloquently on my behalf. Then I got up and asked the judge for an exit visa from the hell in which I had been living for three years.

"I could not die," I said, "nor, however, can I live."

"There is a synonym for misprision," the judge began. "It has achieved a melancholy prominence in recent years. The word is cover-up."

That's it, I thought, *I have been linked to Watergate. Three years in jail.*

But the judge had moved on to a philosophical discussion of three different types of crime: violent and venal, nonviolent but venal, and nonviolent and nonvenal. Then he proceeded to define my own.

"I perceive in this case nothing more and nothing less than human frailty," said the judge.

The tears sprang to my eyes. This man had understood that I was not a criminal.

"Judging by method and by motive," he continued, "your acts are less rather than more severe. Your awareness of wrongdoing was quick, and your remorse complete."

He certainly is generous, I thought. My awareness and remorse were of rather recent vintage.

"I perceive no need for personal punishment greater than that already visited on you. A term of imprisonment is entirely inappropriate."

No jail, I thought with relief, and looked at David. The young lawyer squeezed my hand.

"Wait," he said. "The judge is not yet through."

The black-robed man glanced up from his notes and looked at me.

"Our campuses," he said, "are frequently illuminated by the cold brilliance of scholars. Less frequently the lives of their students are warmed by a teacher's human compassion. I see that factor in this case."

It was true, I thought, *I do care for my students.* There had been an outpouring of sympathy for me, and dozens of my former students had written letters to the judge on my behalf.

"There are minds confined in prison that swing from apathy to frustration to despair," the judge continued. "I am satisfied that useful work can be done among the inmates of a teacher of your gifts."

My God, I thought, *he* will *sentence me to teach in jail.*

"Accordingly," said the judge, "you are to teach in prison for an average time of two hours a week for eighteen months."

I sprang to my feet. "Your Honor," I said with genuine emotion, "it will be a privilege to serve those less fortunate than myself." The words had come out of me spontaneously. The judge's words had moved me deeply.

The black-robed man smiled just a little. "It is my hope," he said, "that this nightmare is now over and that as a result of this program, good may come to others, so that we may achieve that combination of law and mercy that results in justice, a goal that frequently eludes mankind but for which we must continue to aspire."

David embraced me. "It's over," he said.

As I walked out into the wintry January sun, I was aware of the true nature of my offense. The ancient Greeks had called it hubris—presumptuous ambition. Ironically, most of my writings about world politics had dealt with this pervasive theme. Time and time again, nations throughout history had overreached themselves. Some, like Hitler's Germany or Imperial Japan, had to be destroyed completely. Others, like the United States, had to learn and grow through dreadful suffering. Even the leaders of the world's greatest democratic nation would not change their course in Vietnam until they were shaken and shattered into doing so.

Nations, like men, seemed to learn primarily through trauma and catastrophe.

I, too, had overreached myself. I had used my intelligence not to question the reckless path on which I had embarked, but to rationalize my acts. And now the gods' rough justice had been meted out. But I had been fortunate. Nations bent on self-destruction seldom had a second chance. Their course toward oblivion usually proved irreversible. This was the challenge of history, and its tragedy. It was the shape "destiny" assumed on earth. But if I gave up my illusions and my hubris, I could still stop the engine of destruction.

Not surprisingly, my Laura Larrabee debacle had a serious impact on my professional and social life. My speaking engagements dried up noticeably, with a grave consequence for my income. Moreover, I was no longer invited by people whom I thought of as my friends. Even my old mentor, Hans Morgenthau, made himself scarce for several months, despite being a friend to Mary Ann as well as me. It was icy in the house—again—but Mary Ann was sure this scandal would change me once and for all, and so she stayed with me. One notable exception to the desertion of my friends was Elie Wiesel, who would later win the Nobel Peace Prize, and his wife Marion. I had met Elie Wiesel in the 1960s at a series of lectures he gave at Boston University. I approached him after the first class and discovered we had much in common. We became friends. He and his wife maintained an abiding, nonjudgmental friendship that helped me begin the slow process of rebuilding my life. Their encouragement of my plans to teach in prison also helped me to restore my confidence. In short, they were there for me during the worst time of my adult life. For this, they have my undying gratitude.

I resolved to grasp the opportunity to rebuild my life. Within a week, I had worked out a plan whereby, twice a week, I would offer a college course in world politics to a group of federal prisoners. Those who passed a final examination would earn regular college credit. This opportunity, I thought, might give the prisoners new hope and self-esteem, things I was hoping to get back. My plan was approved by the university, and shortly afterward it was endorsed by the warden of a federal penitentiary not far from New York City. An innovative and exciting way to use my teaching talent had suddenly opened up. I sensed this new prison course might soon develop into a lasting professional commitment.

The myth of Eden records the painful fact that each person must leave his garden of illusion to become fully human. The overtones of woe with which this myth has echoed down the ages testify to the reluctance and the pain with which wisdom—and hence full humanity—is born. Perhaps my new assignment would be the beginning of such wisdom.

There had been an escape from the New York Metropolitan Prison a week before commencement and the guards were nervous. The fugitive had used one of the bathrooms to change his prison denims into street clothes that his girlfriend had brought during a visit. Then he had simply walked out of the building with the rest of the visitors. Since then, the guards counted the five hundred inmates four times every day.

A guard appeared and motioned me to follow him. The walk to the prison classroom was a long and tedious one since we had to traverse a number of empty cells, all of which had to be unlocked and then locked again. My escort was overweight and in no particular hurry as he slammed the cell doors shut, testing each lock carefully.

"Big night tonight, eh?" he asked.

"That's right," I answered. I had been teaching the college course in world politics to a group of prisoners during the past year and this was the night of their final examination. The members of the class had been selected by the warden and I had donated the books.

"Think they'll make it?" asked the turnkey. I noticed a trace of irritation in his voice. "I never got to go to college," he continued. "But nowadays the crooks get themselves a college education."

We had reached the classroom and the guard locked the door behind me. I was alone with my students in a federal penitentiary. During the first few weeks, it had made me slightly edgy to be locked up with a group of criminals, even though a guard was usually posted outside the classroom. As the months passed, however, my fear had vanished. I had grown to like my new students and sensed they appreciated what I had to offer. Gradually, I became involved and began to look forward to my two evenings a week in jail. Frequently, I stayed on after class and talked to the inmates individually. Now that a year had passed, I had come to know them well and to care for some of them quite deeply.

I looked over the class and saw that all nine were there. At the beginning, there had been twenty, but eleven had been transferred to other penal institutions during the year, almost always without warning. When I complained about this practice to a prison official on one occasion, he looked at me with a thin smile and said, "It may be your course, Professor, but it's our jail." There was no malice in his voice, only the indifference of an overburdened bureaucrat.

One of my students, a fifty-five-year-old man who had already served fifteen years of a life sentence, passed out the examination booklets.

"Looks tough," said Claire, looking over the questions. I knew she was joking. Claire was the twenty-six-year-old daughter of a college professor from Colorado. She already had two degrees and was the best student in the class. Two years earlier, Claire had fallen in love with a Croat nationalist while studying in Vienna and had married him after a brief courtship. The Croat had agitated for years against the Communist government that was ruling his homeland, but no one in power had paid the slightest attention to him. Finally, in a fit of frenzy, the young man had hijacked a passenger plane and forced the pilot to fly halfway around the world to attract attention to his cause. He had informed his wife a few days before the hijacking and she had desperately tried to dissuade him. At the last moment, fearing for her husband's life, Claire went along with him and passed out leaflets among the passengers. The thought of reporting the man she loved to the authorities had never even occurred to her. When the plane ran out of fuel and landed in London, the couple surrendered and was promptly extradited to the United States. A jury found the young Croat and his wife guilty of air piracy resulting in a death. As it turned out, the man had left a bomb behind in a railroad station locker and a police officer was killed while attempting to dismantle the explosive. Claire had maintained at her trial that she had not known about the bomb, but the jury had not believed her story.

I remembered my conversations with my attorney about going to trial in my own case and that he had counseled against it. I began to understand with sadness that there was a great deal more to our criminal justice system than met the eye, and that law and justice were not necessarily the same.

Both Claire and her husband were given mandatory life sentences, and now they were to be shipped to different prisons. Claire still loved her husband and her one request to me had been that he be permitted to attend the commencement ceremony I had arranged for those students who would pass the course. She had only just begun to grasp the enormity of her predicament.

"My God," she had gasped when she was told of her husband's imminent transfer. "They will destroy my marriage. I will never have children; I'll be an old woman when I get out!"

I was unable to disagree, so I kept silent. But the thought that a vibrant young woman who had made one tragic, terrible mistake should be buried alive made me feel sick. When I had suggested to a prison official that justice would be better served if Claire were allowed to hold a regular job under psychiatric supervision, but donated most of her income for twenty years to the dead policeman's family, the man had merely laughed.

"I don't think the American people would stand for that," he had said.

"Would the American people prefer to pay a quarter of a million for her twenty-year incarceration?" I had asked.

Shortly after her conviction, she had written a thoughtful paper on terrorism, pointing out that some terrorists had become prime ministers of the very states for whose nationhood they had fought. While I had serious doubts about Claire's point that only a thin line divided the terrorist from the patriot, I admired her loyalty to the man she loved. She was a forthright, honest person who had fallen in love with a self-destructive, misguided idealist. Now she employed her entire intelligence to rationalize her husband's deed, which had cost another human being's life. Her sanity, no doubt, depended on her ability to maintain this rationalization. She would probably serve her sentence in a spirit of martyrdom for a cause that had meant absolutely nothing to her before the fateful meeting with her desperate lover.

Saul, another of the inmates, was looking nervously around the room. He had forgotten his pen again and now there was no way to get out. Ten locked doors separated him from his ballpoint. I lent him mine and he looked at me gratefully. Saul had been a successful lawyer, but had been disbarred and convicted for having sold swampland in Florida to prospective real estate investors. Even though he had made complete restitution to the victims of the land swindle and had gone into bankruptcy to make amends, the judge had taken a dim view of a lawyer running afoul of the law and had given Saul three years. Saul was doing hard time, as the prison jargon put it. He was a compulsive worker and was terrified of idleness. He assisted the rabbi with Sabbath services on Friday nights and the priest with church services on Sunday mornings. During the week, he worked as a clerk in the warehouse and in his spare time he prepared parole applications for other prisoners. At night, he did push-ups or scrubbed his cell. He could not face the fact that he was serving time in jail and that the stigma would remain with him after his release.

"Prison," he said to me once, "is a place of dehabilitation, not of rehabilitation. Do you know," he asked me, "what it costs to keep me here a year?" I shook my head. "Fifteen thousand dollars!" Saul shouted. "I am not a violent man," he continued. "Would it not have made more sense to let me work for nothing for the Legal Aid Society for three years instead of locking me up and wasting my skill and your money?"

I found it difficult to disagree with Saul and his concept of service rather than imprisonment. But when I mentioned the idea to a correction officer, he, too, dismissed it with a laugh. "That wouldn't be much of a punishment," he said. The economics of Saul's argument made no impression on him. He was just one of many prison officials who expressed a need for revenge and punishment.

It also became clear to me that prison was a business and a supplier of a variety of jobs. I wondered, though, as I looked at Saul scribbling furiously on his pad, what would become of him after his release. He would never again be permitted to practice his profession. What would his two children think of him? Would the stigma of disbarment and a prison record seduce him back into another shady deal?

I was interrupted in my thoughts by Charles, who was rising from his chair. He was a large man with bladder trouble and I knew that he had to go to the bathroom. This had posed a problem on numerous occasions during the year. Despite the fact that there was a bathroom adjacent to the class, the quick-change escape artist still haunted the guards. The only way to obtain the key was to knock at the door and hope that a guard would hear. Charles was lucky. Two soft taps at the door summoned Angelo, who promptly opened the bathroom door for Charles. "How's it going?" he whispered. Angelo had sat in on a couple of my sessions, but had found the material too difficult and had quietly withdrawn. Nonetheless, he was never jealous or bitter. He was always pleasant and considerate, and whenever he was on duty, I could be sure that the class would not be held up by wasteful and arbitrary delays.

Not all the guards were as courteous as Angelo. One particularly nasty type had kept me waiting once in the prison lobby for two hours only to tell me finally with thinly disguised relish that he wouldn't let me in at all. My protest that this was my regular teaching night had only offended his authority. "This is not the street," he said. "I'll give you one minute to get out. Now git!" I left without another word. A letter of complaint I wrote to the warden afterward got no response.

Charles, visibly relieved, emerged from the bathroom and lumbered back toward his seat. He was serving a one-year sentence for stock fraud. He and Saul were friends although Saul resented the fact that Charles had drawn a lighter sentence for a comparable crime. The subject of different sentences for similar crimes was an unending topic of conversation between the two men. Charles was desperately ashamed of being in jail and had forbidden his wife to visit him. His friends and associates had been told that he was on an extended business trip. As the date of his release approached, Charles was terrified lest the truth about him became known and ruin him in the community. Unable to face that prospect, he was fast sinking into a depression. Freedom to him was a terrible moment of truth when society might discover that he was a criminal.

Angelo lit up a cigarette as he prepared to leave the classroom. Leroy sniffed the air and made a pleading gesture toward Angelo. The guard walked over and handed the prisoner his half-empty pack. Leroy was a bank robber who had already served nine years of a twenty-year sentence. He had taken the course to have a better chance when he went before the parole board within the coming year. He had a wife and ten-year-old daughter who lived in a tenement in Harlem. It had taken Leroy half a year to open up to me a little.

"Do you ever see your wife?" I asked him once.

"Yeah, but we are not allowed to be alone," Leroy answered bitterly. "Sometimes I wish the bastards had castrated me," he continued vehemently. "I am only thirty."

Leroy had escaped five years ago and then police had found him the next day at home in bed with his wife. Three more years were added to his sentence. Since then, Leroy's rage knew no bounds. But he understood that he had to sit on constant guard duty of his emotions. He had to resist the urge to take offense, to escape, to revolt, or to fight back because another mistake would put him back at square one. "You can't fight 'em," he said in a heavy voice.

He counted time from one Christmas to another because he was allowed to spend that day with his wife and daughter. Leroy yearned to make love to his young wife and worried about other men.

"They won't let a man be with his wife but they don't care about homosexuality in jail," he said.

Time to him was like a meter, adding the years, implacably. He had done well in my course and had overcome serious deficiencies in basic education. His entire life was fixated on the obligatory ten-minute interview with the parole board, now only another year away.

"I've got to pass this course, Doc," he said to me almost every week.

I had no doubt that he would. His fellow students told me that Leroy was no longer available for cards or Ping-Pong after work. He studied in his cell at least three hours every night.

I looked at my watch. Almost half of the time allotted for the examination had passed. The classroom was completely silent. My eye fell on Smokey, who was cleaning out his pipe. It was almost always in his mouth but I had never actually seen him smoke. Smokey was a lifer who was somewhat of a mystery. He had done fifteen years in different penal institutions and had been transferred a year ago to the prison where I taught my course. A man of considerable intellect and erudition, he chose not to speak about himself, nor did I find it appropriate to question him. Our conversations remained limited to abstract topics, usually philosophical in nature. Smokey's favorite subject was the complex nature of justice. He found it inexhaustible. Once, after a particularly lively dialogue, however, Smokey did let down his reserve.

"Doc," he said, reaching for my hand, "I wish I could do something for you, too."

I was so surprised that I couldn't think of anything to say. I simply shook his hand without a word.

The prison rumor had it that fifteen years earlier, Smokey had been involved in a violent crime, but no one seemed to be familiar with the specific circumstances of the case. Now, Smokey seemed much older than fifty-five years. I saw no trace of the violence that had been responsible for the ruination of his life. His health was failing and his complexion had a waxen and unhealthy look. Twice during the past hour he had shuffled over to the water cooler for a drink. He was about to rise for yet another trip but didn't seem to have the strength. Quickly, I filled a paper cup with water and took it over to his seat. "Thanks, Doc," Smokey whispered gratefully. "I don't know what's the matter with me tonight."

A wave of sympathy for the aging man came over me as I walked back to my chair. *Why had I permitted myself to become so involved?* I asked myself for the one-hundredth time. After all, none of my students in this class was innocent. I could not come up with a simple answer. The rebel in me was appalled by the indifference and arbitrariness of the prison authorities. There seemed to be little if any emphasis on rehabilitation. Most individual expression was crushed by a relentless, impersonal bureaucracy.

It was also true, however, that the students were appreciative and considerate. Every time I appeared, the blackboard was scrubbed clean and one of the inmates handed me a piece of chalk. "We've been waiting for you all week," he said sincerely. I sensed that many of these men and women had not experienced kindness or respect in many years and had learned to bury their emotions well. But when they felt that someone took a genuine interest, their need for warmth quickly broke down their defenses. After half a year, I had found my prison teaching to be so meaningful that I was prepared to make it a permanent commitment. I knew that had I been less fortunate, I, too, might have wound up here. In fact, every time I left the jail, late at night, I felt a pang of guilt. A less empathetic or understanding judge could have ruined my life without redemption. But the opportunity to teach in prison, to use my talent rather than rot in jail, had given a new meaning to my life. Dimly, I perceived that my selfish striving for success had somehow always left me empty. I never felt this emptiness when I met my prison class. My human value had undergone a transformation.

I looked over at Smokey. He seemed to have recovered and was absorbed again in the examination. In one of our many conversations, Smokey had maintained that no man was really competent to judge another. He found the inequity in sentencing procedures among different judges appalling and capricious. My reply that greater uniformity in sentencing probably was in the offing left Smokey totally unsatisfied.

"Doc," he said with emphasis, "society must learn to differentiate between the offense and the offender."

"But what about equality before the law?" I managed to retort.

"After all these years," Smokey answered thoughtfully, "I have finally come up with a definition of a criminal."

"And what is that?" I asked, intensely curious.

"A criminal," Smokey said after a lengthy pause, "is someone who destroys himself."

I was so perplexed by this definition that, for a long time, I said nothing. It soon occurred to me, however, that there was a profound logic in Smokey's answer. Each of the prisoners in my class had engaged in a self-destructive act that had landed him in jail. I knew many people who were free outside whom I would consider morally inferior to many of my prison students. But those people had simply not been caught. They had refused to self-destruct. No wonder I had often sensed with some surprise that the moral quality of prison inmates did not seem to differ very sharply from that of the society that put them there. Smokey's definition of a criminal would probably not appear in any text on criminology, but I thought he had a point.

I was jarred out of my thoughts by a jangling of keys outside the classroom. The door opened abruptly and a strident voice barked, "Everett!" It was Miss Powell, a particularly aggressive woman guard who apparently took pleasure in yanking prisoners out of my class to assert her authority.

"Miss Powell," I said quietly, barely able to conceal my anger, "Tim Everett is taking a final examination."

Miss Powell looked at me with a blank stare.

"Orders from the lieutenant," she snapped. "Some lights need fixing."

I decided not to protest any further. If I provoked her, Miss Powell would probably throw me out. Tim Everett followed her obediently out the door.

"Please try to bring him back as soon as possible," I asked, but Miss Powell simply locked the door without another word.

Tim Everett was an English engineer who loved the sea. He was also a hashish smuggler who regarded his trade not only as a lucrative source of income but also as a form of high adventure. His sloop had outrun the United States Coast Guard and a faster ship had chased him all the way down to Bermuda, where he was finally taken into custody. The United States had demanded extradition and the British had complied. Tim had been in jail a year and was known as Mr. Fixit among the prison staff. A first-class engineer, he was able to repair almost any mechanical malfunction. If anything went wrong in the metal entrails of the prison apparatus, Tim would quickly make a diagnosis and prescribe the proper cure. In his spare time, he liked to listen to classical music. Rumor had it that he had attended the Royal Naval College at Dartmouth. A self-contained man, he spoke sparingly.

"What will you do when you get out?" I asked him once.

"I'll go back to the sea," said Tim without a moment's hesitation. Something told me not to pursue the subject further. I suspected that Tim would quickly resume his favorite trade.

Rachel, who had been sitting next to Tim, had a pained expression on her face. Like Tim, she did not speak much and I knew very little about her. She was in prison on a charge of contempt for refusing to testify against her lover, who was in the narcotics importing business. Rachel had appeal despite a rough, common exterior, and one could easily imagine her in a long mink coat rather than her orange prison suit. Whenever I brought food into the prison to be shared by my students after class, she usually helped herself to the largest portion. On one occasion, I had brought in a quiche lorraine. Rachel sniffed at it and then recoiled in horror.

"It's got ham in it," she said. "I can't eat it. I am Jewish." In the end, however, unable to resist, she had helped herself to a large slice, which she munched without a trace of guilt.

"I'll tell you a story," she said, laughing at my puzzled look, "why I ate the ham. An old rabbi on his deathbed," Rachel began, "asks his son for a ham sandwich. The son is horrified. 'You have lived a holy life,' he berates his father. 'Why do you wish to end it with a sin?' 'On the day of judgment,' the old man answers, 'there will be a prosecuting angel and a defending angel. As you know, the prosecuting angel will tell me which sin each stroke is for. It will hurt a lot and I will pray for the end of the beating to come. And then, when I hear the angel say, "And this is for the ham sandwich," I'll know it's over.'"

Rachel laughed and took the last slice of quiche off the paper plate. "It'll be over for me soon," she said. "I should be out of here in a few weeks."

Rachel hoped to join her lover, who had fled the country, but whose exact whereabouts were unknown. In class, she showed intelligence and humor but seldom expressed opinions. She would do well on the examination, I was sure, but I realized that I had no idea who she really was.

Reggie, I had noticed, had not been writing for almost half an hour. Instead, he was sitting in his chair, head in hand, looking puzzled. Apparently, he had difficulty with one of the questions. I walked over to his seat and placed my hand on his shoulder. Reggie looked up at me, despair written on his face.

"Taps for me," he whispered. "It's too tough."

"No, it's not," I countered. "I want you to keep on writing."

"I'll do my best, Prof," Reggie whispered back, "but I think it's way over my head."

Reggie had been a printer and engraver who was doing time for forgery.

"What are you in for?" I had asked him once.

"Selling treasury bills," he answered.

"What's wrong with that?" I questioned.

"Well," said Reggie, "you see, I printed 'em."

Reggie could have gotten fifteen years but he drew a judge who gave him only three. Two years after his arrival in the jail, Reggie made a commitment to give his life to Christ. He learned dental hygiene in the prison and spent eight hours every day cleaning his fellow inmates' teeth. In his spare time, he studied scripture and served as an unofficial welcoming committee for newly arrived prisoners. He had married a pretty Irish girl just before he was incarcerated. His wife visited him as often as the rules allowed and counted the days until his release. The only thing that worried him was whether he would find a job. Society, he felt, was unforgiving toward former criminals. He doubted whether prospective employers would be prepared to take a chance on him. No intellectual, he had nevertheless worked doggedly to pass my course and the "street smarts" that he displayed during discussion periods had often livened up the class. After a lecture on the Vietnam War, he shook his head and sighed. "I never knew that brilliant people could be that dumb. I stole money, but they stole human lives." I couldn't help but think, listening to Reggie, that all my degrees and all my books had not protected me against Laura Larrabee.

There was much discussion in the jail about Reggie's religious conversion. At first, the news was greeted with skepticism, and even laughter. But now, two years later, most of Reggie's fellow prisoners believed that his new commitment was entirely authentic. I, too, had the feeling that Reggie was sincere.

I glanced over at Omus as I walked back to my chair. I was concerned about him. Omus had come from a broken home in Harlem and had spent most of his life in jail. His career of crime had begun with car theft at the age of seventeen and ten years later he was convicted for armed robbery and given twenty years. In addition, Omus had a record for pushing heroin and had himself succumbed to the addiction. His arms, I had noticed, were full of needle marks. Nevertheless, he had taken remarkable steps toward rehabilitation. He had kicked his habit, had learned to write English, and had earned the equivalent of a high school diploma. He worked in the kitchen and had learned to cook. Jail had become a kind of home to him. When the parole board had turned him down three years ago, he was not the least upset, as the world outside held little promise for him. In jail, he had a clean cell all to himself, plentiful food, and even the chance to educate himself. When I asked him whether he had any family, he shook his head.

"This is my family," he said, pointing to the walls surrounding him.

"What will you do when you get out?" I asked him once after he had displayed considerable knowledge about Africa in class.

"Try to get back in," he said.

I wasn't surprised at this reply. After all, 80 percent of all prisoners who were released sooner or later went back to jail.

I wondered whether he would pass the exam, as his writing skills were only marginal. Yet I was pulling for him since I admired him for his perseverance and his courage.

The two hours allotted for the exam were over and I got up to collect the papers.

"Be good to us," said Reggie as he handed me his examination. I went from chair to chair and gathered up the blue books. Suddenly, a shock went through me. I had looked at Smokey. His face was deathly white and beads of sweat were running down his face.

"Doc," he strained in a tortured whisper, "it's my heart, I think, please help me."

"Guard, guard!" I yelled as I ran to the door, hammering at the locked door with both my fists. There was no response. "Please!" I screamed. "Please open the door!" Silence still. I turned around. Claire and Rachel had lifted Smokey out of his chair and laid him on the floor. His eyes were glazed over and his breathing came in fits and starts. I took off my coat and placed it under Smokey's head. Then I took his hand in both my own.

"Smokey," I said, "try to breathe quietly. We are getting a doctor."

Leroy, panther-like, leapt to the door and scratched at it with his fingernails.

"Doctor, doctor, get a doctor, a man is dying here!" he screamed, totally beside himself. Rachel bent over Smokey and pressed her mouth to his, trying to pump air into his lungs. I wondered where she had picked up her knowledge of first aid. Smokey's chest heaved and suddenly expanded. A tormented gasp escaped from his throat. We had formed a little circle around him. Only Leroy was still clawing at the door.

I caressed Smokey's hand helplessly, and then I saw his eyes open.

"Doc," he said, "I hope I pass the exam."

"Of course you will," I said, and gave his hand a squeeze. I had begun to cry. Smokey, lying on my coat, turned his head toward me with an effort.

"I mean the big exam, the final one," he whispered, and then he closed his eyes.

When the guard finally came, a lifetime later, Smokey's hand had already grown cold.

Commencement was beautiful and sad. A small room had been set aside for the occasion and three inmates had set up a table and some chairs. The table was covered with a green felt cloth dug up by Tim Everett. All of my nine students had passed, but Smokey was already in his grave. The warden did not attend, but had allowed each of my students to invite one family member to the ceremony, including Claire's husband. It was probably the last time the young Croat would see his wife before his transfer to another penitentiary. Claire managed a small smile when she walked up to the table to receive her certificate.

I had not been able to persuade Charles to invite his wife even though he had passed the course with honors. Saul, too, was alone. Leroy, looking proud and angry, was sitting next to his young daughter.

After the ceremony, Rachel prepared a reddish nonalcoholic punch. Homemade chocolate cookies I had brought for the occasion has been confiscated at the gate because someone had forgotten to fill out a special permission slip for the warden's signature. Reggie beamed with pride as he held hands with his young, attractive wife. Omus came up to me and reached for my hand.

"This is the most important piece of paper in my life," he said, pointing to his diploma. He was scheduled to be shipped to Lewisburg the following morning. Omus's written exam had been borderline at best, but I had given him an oral in the hope that he would pass. I was glad now that he had.

Reggie said a prayer for Smokey and we all bowed our heads. I hoped we would remember him. All too quickly, the living closed ranks against the dead. Reggie also said something about a jail commencement being a new beginning. I hoped that he was right. Our little group was about to disperse into a most uncertain future and I would miss the first group of prison students greatly. If I had affected them, they, too, had left their mark on me. But I would continue. Soon I would teach another group of prisoners, and then yet another. I had found a new vocation.

It was Smokey, though, who had left me the most precious gift. His wish had been prophetic. I had held his hand before he died. At his funeral, I had been wracked by sobs that had erupted without warning. I was unable to stop for a long time. Afterward, I felt a quiet sadness that finally gave way to a serenity that I had never known. It became clear to me that I had never had the privilege of mourning. My father had been wrenched out of my life before I fully understood death's meaning. I had blamed myself and the guilt had stayed with me, a child doomed to carry the suicide into manhood. Now, at last, more than four decades later, I stood at my father's burial. Through grieving for Smokey, I also mourned my long-dead father, and finally, I was free.

I taught in prison for more than three years, twice the time required. The president of Hunter College, Mrs. Jacqueline Wexler, a former nun who had left the order and married a Jew, was a profound believer in the possibility of redemption. Not only did she authorize college credit for my inmate students, but she also attended commencement exercises each semester and congratulated the graduates on their progress toward rehabilitation.

I would have continued this program indefinitely had it not been for a "revolt" by prison guards who complained that the prisoners were being "coddled." This is how, to my dismay, my new calling came to an abrupt end. I was bereft because helping the inmates rebuild their lives had given my own life new meaning. Not even a generous letter of appreciation from the sentencing judge or a full pardon granted me by President Ronald Reagan was able to lift me out of a deepening gloom.

Not surprisingly, my favorite project at the City University, the UN institute, was taken over by a colleague. I was also too embarrassed to show my face at the United Nations because of Laura Larrabee's thievery.

To make matters worse, my old mentor Professor Morgenthau's health was failing, and he would show up at our home only infrequently. When he did come, he would lie down on the living room sofa and I would take off his shoes and hold his hand. He died in July 1980, and most of New York's academic elite showed up for the funeral service. Henry Kissinger delivered the eulogy, which he began with the words, "Hans Morgenthau was my teacher." I grieved for Hans, but it was the grief of a man for his older mentor, no longer the despair of a son yearning for his father.

There was yet a far more serious problem. My marriage to Mary Ann was growing cold. The stress that the affair with Laura had placed on our marriage was simply too much for both of us to bear. I tried hard to be a decent husband. I was attentive to my wife, helped in furthering her musical career, and was generous with money. Yet something inside me had gone numb. The fact that she was completely innocent only made matters worse. My self-esteem was simply crushed.

Not surprisingly, Mary Ann's fury had been thoroughly aroused when I left for Texas. She promptly filed for divorce, got herself a first-rate lawyer, and succeeded in stripping me of my entire retirement benefits from Hunter College and from the United Nations.

Since I not only felt guilty, but was in fact guilty, I did not put up much of a fight. I wanted to provide for my wife and our daughter to the very best of my ability. I gave what I was capable of giving—money—for a daughter I seldom got to see, so she could go to the very best New York private schools and an Ivy League university. While Mary Ann's animus was justified, it prevented me from having a relationship with my daughter. Shakespeare's famous quip that hell hath no fury like a woman scorned did not apply here. I never scorned Mary Ann; I just could not deal with marriage. I had not married either one of my two wives of my own volition. They had married me.

I said earlier that I was grateful to have an opportunity to rebuild my life, but I wrestled with who I was as a man, colleagues abandoning me, and a marriage shattered beyond repair. It was at this time in 1978 that I met Janis Lasser, a beautiful, intelligent woman, twenty-one years my junior, a former teacher and television writer in New York. On our first date, I gave her a copy of my latest book and hoped she wouldn't research my name in the library. Today, I would have been "Googled," and I'm sure that would have been our first and last date.

She had never heard of me before, despite all the dirty laundry of the Larrabee affair having been aired in the *New York Times* and *Time* magazine. By 5 a.m., we were closing the last coffee shop, having talked all night. I told her she would be the love of my life and we'd be together for a very long time. Skeptical, she said, "That's all relative in a man's world. A long time could mean twenty-five minutes."

She was wrong.

Twenty-five minutes turned into twenty-five years. Separated from Mary Ann, I moved into Janis's tiny studio apartment on

Central Park West and took her home to meet my mother. My mother called her "Golden Girl," and they formed a bond that was to be of great help to me years later when my mother was diagnosed with Alzheimer's disease.

Life in New York had become difficult for me, but Janis made it bearable. The final straw in my life in New York came when a mugger held me up on Riverside Drive, where I often walked for miles to seek some solace. In 1983, after teaching at New York University, Columbia, and City University of New York, I accepted a position at Trinity University in San Antonio, Texas. I asked Janis to come with me.

A word must be said here about my mother and my stepfather, both of whom had settled in New York during the 1950s when I was a graduate student at Harvard. My stepfather had died in 1963 and I had forgiven him on his deathbed and had thanked him for saving my life from the Nazis. My mother now owned her own little hat store on upper Broadway, near Columbia, where I taught in the School of International Affairs. She had built up quite a clientele and, whenever I showed up at the store after a class, she would introduce me proudly to her customers as her son, "the professor." My mother never missed any of my lectures at the Ethical Culture Society on Central Park West. She loved her work and was completely self-supporting. Gradually, she began to show signs of dementia and one night, a policeman telephoned and reported that my mother had been found wandering around at night near her store, unable to find her way home. I couldn't leave her in New York.

Janis urged me to bring my mother to San Antonio to live with us, and that worked for a while, but her Alzheimer's behaviors were more than I could handle and I asked Janis to find an appropriate place for my mother to live. At that time, there weren't a lot of good choices. "Nice" places didn't want people with "behaviors." By this time, Janis had earned a graduate degree in geriatrics and knew more about this than I cared to know, but I did agree to attend some support meetings.

Before she had been struck down by Alzheimer's, my mother had asked me to find a way to thank the two Japanese diplomats who had helped me in my flight from the Nazis. Both men had disappeared after the war without a trace, yet two questions never ceased to haunt me: Who was the mysterious consul in Prague who gave us the transit visas via Kobe? And why did Dr. Manabe, our companion on the Trans-Siberian Express, put himself at risk to help us stay out of the Jewish ghetto in Shanghai? I promised her I would find the answers, and I began my search.

My mother passed away in 1992; I would not track down these men until two years later.

CHAPTER 10

South Africa, Spring 1994

As some readers of this book may notice, there is a certain symmetry to it in that the beginning and the end deal with the same topic—the evil of racial prejudice and its terrible consequences.

On one of my trips back to New York, I had lunch with a very dear friend from my United Nations days, Mr. Brian Urquhart who was known for his unwavering commitment to the world organization and to Scotland, his home.

"Johnny," he said casually over dessert, "you are still young, you could still do some good, why don't you visit South Africa and help Mr. Mandela avert a civil war? He has just been elected president and he has his hands full. I consider him the greatest statesman in the world."

In the mid-1980s, Janis and I had hosted Prince Mangosuthu Buthelezi of KwaZulu and his wife, Princess Irene, in our home in San Antonio and my interest in South African politics was piqued. Buthelezi founded the Inkatha Freedom Party in 1975 and was a chief of the Zulu royal family. He was ten years Mandela's junior.

I had, of course, heard of Nelson Mandela and had followed his career in the American press. I admired his tireless effort to do away with apartheid, the noxious discrimination imposed by whites against blacks to keep them inferior and without voting rights.

I had a free summer coming up and had never been to South Africa, and so I decided it might be a nice vacation. Little did I know that this trip would have such an impact on my life.

On a beautiful morning in May 1994, I flew on South African Airlines to Johannesburg, with a quick stop on the Azores Islands to take on fuel. From Johannesburg, I took a train to Pretoria, the capital of South Africa, where I had an appointment with the newly elected president. I sat in a modest waiting room for only a few minutes when an attractive African American lady came up to me and asked whether I was the professor from the United States. When I said yes, she quickly replied that the president was expecting me and would see me in less than a few minutes. And indeed, in a few minutes the secretary returned and said politely that the president was ready to welcome me, adding that he was playing a game of soccer with his grandson and hoped that I wouldn't mind.

To say that I was surprised when I was ushered into the president's office would be an understatement.

Here was President Nelson Mandela, sitting on the floor pushing a tiny soccer ball back and forth with one of his fingers. Also on the floor sat a little boy, about four years old, trying to push the ball past his grandfather into a tiny goal. When Mr. Mandela turned around, he noticed my presence and rose quickly from the floor to shake my hand. He did this with amazing speed and agility, not at all like a man in his eighties.

"Come in and sit down, Dr. John, and play soccer with us, it's our favorite game."

I noticed that he wore a beautiful velvet robe and sandals.

"This robe is a gift from my fiancée; I have to get some new sandals," he said. His sandals had fallen off and revealed that he was wearing socks. I couldn't help but notice that both socks had big holes in them, right down the middle.

"Dr. John," he said apologetically, "I have no one to darn my socks; I am in the middle of a divorce."

"So am I, Mr. President," I replied, "I have no one to darn my socks, either." It was true: first Julie and then Mary Ann. I was simply no good at marriage and had no one to blame but myself.

I couldn't help but wonder why I confided in Nelson Mandela. After all, he was a perfect stranger. And yet he read my mind.

"I do not judge you, Dr. John," said the president, "but I would like to be your friend. How long can you stay with us? I would like you to hear my inaugural address. Tomorrow I must take the Blue Train to Cape Town as I have some appointments there. Why don't you come with me, so that I can show you our beautiful South Africa from the train?"

Needless to say, I agreed, and I was amply rewarded. Crossing South Africa by train was like experiencing the book of Genesis from the Old Testament. I saw lions, tigers, and tall giraffes that stretched their long necks to grab the food given to them by Nelson Mandela, who had requested that the train slow down.

"I like animals," Mr. Mandela said. "They never lie. Have you noticed that they live together in peace? Like in Genesis," he added. He had read my mind again.

As the train approached Cape Town, I told Mandela about my youth under the Nazis.

"Have you been able to forgive Hitler?" he asked me.

I began to stutter. "Only God can do that; I can't," I replied.

"Good answer," the president replied.

On his inauguration day in Pretoria, May 10, 1994, I was given a seat in one of the front rows. I saw Mr. F. W. de Klerk sworn in as vice president. Then President Nelson Mandela rose from his seat and spoke the following words:

> It was during these long and lonely years in prison that the hunger for my own people became a hunger for the freedom of all people, white and black. I know in my heart that the oppressor must be liberated just as surely as the oppressed. I am not truly free if I am taking away someone else's freedom. The oppressor and the oppressed alike are robbed of their humanity. We have not taken the final step of our journey, but the first step on a longer and more difficult road. For, to be free is not merely to cast off one's chains, but to live in a way that respects and enhances the freedom of others. The true test of our devotion to freedom is just beginning. Let freedom reign. God bless Africa!

When it was time to say good-bye, I gave him an inscribed copy of my book, *Why Nations Go to War*. He gave me a bear hug and embraced me, saying, "Dr. John, I admire you. You are not just a writer, but also a fighter against the evil in the world. I have decided to write an autobiography entitled *Long Walk to Freedom*. I will send you a copy."

President Nelson Mandela ruled South Africa for two four-year terms. By the end of these eight years, apartheid had disappeared, not by violence and oppression, but by his example. Mandela was considered to be the founding father of a new democratic government on the African continent, the Republic of South Africa.

The book he said he would write, *Long Walk to Freedom*, now occupies a place of honor in my library. It is a worldwide bestseller.

One of Mandela's most significant contributions during his presidency was the creation of several Truth and Reconciliation Commissions that traveled throughout South Africa. The procedure was simple but highly effective. A large audience was invited to listen to people, mostly white, who had committed injustices against blacks and who wanted to confess and be forgiven. The audience was then asked to consider whether these confessions were sincere and whether they deserved forgiveness. After often vigorous discussions, the audience made its decision by democratic vote. The distinctive feature of this procedure was that it was not a legal process; the words "crime" and "punishment" were not applicable.

I have no doubt that these "Commissions" will long outlive their creator as an outstanding contribution to peace in the world.

During the summer of 2013, the ninety-four-year-old Mandela fell ill. Death claimed this bravest of men in December 2013 at the age of ninety-five.

As for me, I will always remember Madiba's now famous words: "Never forget that forgiveness is the greatest of the virtues. It sets us free!"

CHAPTER 11

Japan, Fall 1994

Having returned from South Africa, I was invited to give a speech in Kobe, Japan, the very city I had transited as a refugee from Hitler half a century before.

Toward the end of my speech in Kobe, I told the story of my flight from Hitler and asked the assembled press corps to help me find the two Japanese diplomats who had saved me so that I could thank them for my life.

That night, the phone rang in my hotel room. It was Mr. Toshinori Masuno of the *Kobe Shimbun*, a leading Japanese newspaper.

"We found out how you got your visas," the reporter said. "It was Consul Chiune Sugihara who issued thousands of visas to Jewish refugees against the express orders of his superiors in Tokyo." This had to be the man who asked me as a little boy if I could speak Japanese—the man to whom I had said, "Hai. Banzai!"

I began to tremble. I wondered whether this was a Japanese Oskar Schindler or Raoul Wallenberg.

"Sugihara issued most of these visas in Lithuania until they posted him to Prague in early 1941," Masuno continued. "And the three of you were on the list. You were among the last before they shut down his consulate."

"Why did he do it?" I inquired.

"He saw this as a conflict between his government and his conscience," the reporter replied, "and he followed his conscience."

"When did he die?" I asked.

"In 1986, in disgrace for not having followed orders," Masuno said sadly. "But he was a moral hero in Israel. They planted a tree in his honor in Jerusalem."

"And what about Dr. Manabe?" I queried.

"We are still searching," the reporter replied. "But he's probably deceased."

That night I returned to the United States to teach my classes. *Too late,* I thought. *I cannot thank either one of them; it's too late.*

The next morning, the phone woke me from a troubled sleep. It was Mr. Masuno again.

"We've found Dr. Manabe!" he exclaimed. "He is eighty-seven years old and quite frail, but he remembers everything. He lives alone and has an unlisted phone number. We managed to get it for you, though."

I thought of little else that day, November 16, 1994. And then, in the middle of the night, the middle of his day, I dialed the number.

He did indeed remember everything. We were not the only ones he had helped more than fifty years ago; other desperate Jews had benefited from his selfless generosity.

A music lover, he had come to the rescue of the Shanghai Philharmonic Orchestra by saving its Jewish members from the ghetto. We both tried not to weep as we recalled those far-gone events, which seemed to have taken place on another planet and in another era. I sent him one of my books, which I would never have written without him, and a picture of my mother taken a year before her death.

Janis faithfully visited my mother in the nursing home, as I couldn't bear it when her Alzheimer's made her physically unrecognizable and combative, and she no longer knew who I was. Only Janis, Janis's mother, and a rabbi were at my mother's graveside service when she was buried in New Jersey. I couldn't bring myself to go. So it was fitting that Janis would urge me to go and see Dr. Manabe for my mother's sake and do for her in death what I didn't do for her in life. She was right, and together we made two trips to see Dr. Manabe. Making our way to the outskirts of Tokyo, to the small apartment where he lived surrounded by his books and a shrine to his late wife, we found a man with a deeply spiritual face, natural grace, and dignity. Bridging half a century proved surprisingly easy. He, like me, had chosen an academic life after the war and had served as a professor of German literature at Tokai University in Tokyo.

We saw each other every day for a week, and I quickly grew to love him. On my last day in Tokyo, I finally asked the question that had always haunted me.

"Weren't you ever afraid to help us?" I asked. "After all, you could have lost your job, or worse, they could have killed you."

He looked at me in amazement. "It was the right thing to do, wasn't it?" he answered, without a moment's hesitation.

I hugged him, and by so doing, had the privilege to express my gratitude to one of the true moral heroes of our time and to do so while he was still alive. Most of us who carry such unredeemable debts must somehow try to honor them after our benefactors' deaths. But I was given the chance to do so in the here and now. Before we left, Janis and I were invited by Makoto Otsuka, general director of the Holocaust Education Center in Fukuyama, to take a private tour of his museum. We were surprised to see this beautiful tribute facility only forty-five miles outside Hiroshima. They had a small ceremony as I planted a tree in their memorial garden. We toured a nearby school where the children were studying Anne Frank and saw how the Japanese "Never Again" education remains vital to this day.

Upon returning to the United States, I realized that I had to teach a most important truth: that there was no such thing as collective guilt, and that, in dark times, there were always men and women who would confront evil, even in its most absolute form, and thereby reaffirm our common humanity. In the depth of the abyss, moral courage still survives and, at times, even prevails.

Dr. Manabe passed away on April 19, 1996.

Janis encouraged me to maintain a relationship with both my children—my son, whom I had with Julie, and my daughter, whom I shared with Mary Ann—but I was never going to be a good father. Janis kept up communication with my dear friend Rusty and his wife in Australia, Uncle Edi and Lola in Vienna, and my cousins in Israel and Switzerland, stressing the importance of family for me. She tried to get me into a synagogue with her but, after the first time, I refused to go back. I wasn't religious. I wasn't even spiritual. I wasn't comfortable in that setting. I was fortunate to have had three good women in my life—Julie, Mary Ann, and Janis—each of whom would have given me a wonderful life if I had been a different kind of man, but I was never going to change. I was no stranger to the squandering of fortunes and opportunities.

While Janis and I traveled the world together and she helped me through triple bypass heart surgery, I could not give up the game. I would never be faithful to anyone. Maybe Oskar's predictions about how I would end would come to pass in the end. I again had an endless stream of simultaneous, meaningless affairs using my past to justify my behaviors, a behavior pattern that I took with me to my next life in San Diego. I believed I needed to have many to love, since all those I loved as a boy had been torn from my life, never to be seen again. Other Holocaust survivors had families and treasured them. Why couldn't I? A teacher and philosopher, Socrates said the unexamined life is not worth living. As I write this in my late eighties, I must believe that it is never too late to examine and reflect.

CHAPTER 12

California, 2000s

As the nineties came to an end, I had developed serious prob-lems at Trinity University. Mary Ann had decided to sue the university and forced it to attach my salary. No amount of money seemed to be enough for her. Finally, in an effort to resolve the problem, I decided to sign over to her my entire retirement from Trinity, the result of fifteen years of teaching, and to call it quits. In June 2000, I moved to California to accept a job offer at the University of San Diego.

Of all the cities in America, and I have seen most of them, San Diego was the loveliest. Its graceful harbor, nestled against an unpretentious skyline, invited the visitor to walk and to explore. A temperate climate without excessive heat or cold was a welcome relief after the stifling heat of Texas. It was wonderful to take a walk without having to wait in line to cross a street, as was the custom in New York, or to look in vain for a taxi in a driving rain or snowstorm.

I explored San Diego for the first time after a speaking engage-ment there in 1990. I had been fascinated by a group of elegant buildings on top of a hill overlooking the bay, and when I had arrived there after an exhilarating hike, I was rewarded with an amazing sight. I was looking at the loveliest university campus I had ever seen. Two Moorish structures dominated a mile-long walkway lined with palm trees.

Since my first visit, I had discovered they had developed an Institute for Peace and Justice next to a church that noted the passing of the hours with silvery chimes. The overall impression of the campus was one of gentleness.

I decided to enter the administration building and, mustering all my chutzpah, walked up to the receptionist, a kind-looking white-haired lady.

"May I see the president, please?" I asked.

"And who are you?" the lady wanted to know, not surprisingly.

I introduced myself and, after one more quizzical look, she asked me to take a seat and wait. Five minutes later, a tall distinguished gentleman with white hair appeared and walked toward me.

"Please come in," he said with a courtly gesture. "Some of our professors are using your books here. What can I do for you?"

"Could you use a Jewish professor at the University of San Diego?" I asked, using up all of my remaining chutzpah.

The president threw back his head and laughed. "Let me telephone the dean," he said, "and we'll see."

The dean of arts and science turned out to be a political scientist as well as a tennis player. He offered me the opportunity to teach a course titled Crisis Areas in World Politics, and I gratefully accepted his offer.

Janis remained in Texas and I moved to San Diego. My first year of teaching at the University of San Diego passed serenely. I looked forward to every class and developed a keen interest in the welfare of my students. Most evenings I sat on the deck of my new home and watched one glorious sunset after another. But then came the horror of September 11, 2001.

For my students, that event was an evil so enormous that it defied imagination. That week, I decided to distribute the words of Schiller's "Ode to Joy," which Beethoven had set to music in the concluding chorale of his Ninth Symphony. Then I copied it and sang it for them.

"If Beethoven found the courage to write this, being completely deaf," I said, "you can find the courage to sing it, especially now!" They did, at first tentatively and then, by the third time, full throttle. There were hugs all around. Beethoven had given us not only courage, but also hope and joy. To survive in a world of so much darkness, young people needed more than academic learning. They also needed love and affirmation.

Then, in early 2002, I was confronted with another health crisis. I contracted a severe case of shingles that had not only settled in my left eye but also affected my eyesight permanently.

My doctor told me in no uncertain terms that he would not allow me to live alone. The pain, he warned, might become unbearable, and I would need care around the clock. If this was unavailable, he would send me to a hospital. Time was of the essence, he added. I would have to decide that very day.

I ruled out the hospital immediately, but did not have a woman friend in California whom I knew well enough to entrust with such a task. I decided to call Rosalinda Gonzalez, a gentle woman with a loving nature I had met in San Antonio.

When I called her and asked whether she could come to San Diego to take care of me, she offered to be on the next plane.

The next six months were an ordeal I would not have survived without Rosalinda. I did not know such pain existed. It felt like an anthill resided in my head that I couldn't get to. Ugly scabs appeared on my face and I was so weak that I could barely walk.

After the contagious phase had passed, I insisted that Rosalinda drive me to the university so that I could meet my classes. Teaching was like therapy for me. I will never forget the kindness of my students when I walked in and my face resembled a bad Picasso painting. I had to sit down to deliver my lectures and, after class, some of the students would take me by the arm and walk me around the campus so that I could get some exercise. All I could eat for dinner was lukewarm soup, and in the evenings Rosalinda would take me for a walk and then she would hold me so that I could get through the night. Often I couldn't stifle a scream when the pain became unbearable.

I recovered slowly. The pain subsided, but never disappeared entirely. The doctors had a fancy name for this aftermath—postherpetic neuralgia—and informed me that I might have to live with it for the rest of my life. Thick sunglasses were prescribed because exposure to the sun could reactivate the virus. This meant that one of my greatest pleasures, sitting in the sun on my deck, was over for good. Instead, as my strength began to return, I made it a daily habit to take long walks after sunset to get my body back in shape.

Rosalinda had rescued me so I decided to rescue her back. She had never had the chance to get a formal education, but her dream was college for her children. I decided to help with their college education and they were soon on their way. Rosalinda repaid me one year later when I choked on a large pill. She performed the Heimlich maneuver in the nick of time. A few seconds more and I think I would have been gone. When Rosalinda fell on her knees afterward to thank God, I felt a surge of love and gratitude. The following day, we both said a prayer of thanks in the church on the university campus.

Just as I was getting back to a normal routine of teaching and writing, the worst was yet to come. Julie's and my son, Richard, who was gay, had contracted HIV in the mid-eighties. For years, his condition had been stable and he was able to do productive work in a film studio in Hollywood. Through him, I had learned that homosexuals were born that way and therefore had no choice about their sexuality. I had also learned that their emotions were no different from those of heterosexuals. They experienced love with the same joy and the same suffering as other people. My son reinforced my own nonjudgmental approach to the human condition and I accepted and loved him without reservation. Then, suddenly, his condition worsened and a life-and-death struggle began as he developed active AIDS. Doctors administered various experimental drugs and "cocktails," but the virus mutated and became immune to all of them. Despite steady emotional support from both his mother and me, the battle for his life was lost. My son, Richard, to whom I had dedicated my book *Why Nations Go to War* since its first publication in 1974, through nine consecutive editions over a period of thirty years, died on July 11, 2005. I had lived in total denial until the end, thinking he would prevail. Only when I realized that the tenth edition, if there was to be one, would have to be dedicated to his memory, did the terrible truth sink in. I had lost my only son.

In my grief, I reached out to those I loved and who loved me. There was Rosalinda, who held me through the nights again. There was Janis, who was writing a brilliant book on American nursing homes. Miraculously, I also reconnected with Susi, from whom I had parted at the Prague railroad station a lifetime earlier. And Eva, my favorite professor's daughter whom I had loved during my days at Harvard, had reappeared in my life like a blessing and I reestablished my special relationship with her.

I remembered how, more than half a century earlier, I did not want a son. Now I had fought like a lion for his life, and yet he had been taken from me. Was this what the ancient Greeks called the "rough justice of the gods"?

My daughter was an innocent casualty of my troubled times when I fled my marriage, even though I found a loving wife. I tried hard, years later, to be a father to her by actively encouraging her remarkable gift for poetry, yet I failed in this attempt. Somehow, we were never able to establish a meaningful emotional connection, probably because it had taken me too long to try. Thus, I was punished by never finding joy in children of my own. Instead, my students became my children and I did my best to help as many of them as I could over the decades. This, too, brought me joy and satisfaction.

Life had finally beaten the hubris out of me. I was no longer interested in fame or power. I was committed now to making contributions by helping others, especially my students and those around me whom I loved. Nor did I care about property or money because all of that was destined to "go into the box," so to speak, at the end.

I had been very fortunate. I had survived the Holocaust and was living a good life in Southern California, doing what I loved to do. But not unlike Job, I still had serious questions to ask of God. If God was all benevolent, and absolute evil like the Holocaust had happened, he could not be all powerful. And if he was all powerful, he could not be all good, since absolute evil clearly did exist. And if he was neither all good nor all powerful, why call him God?

For many years, I had struggled with this conundrum without finding any answers in the accepted norms of organized religion. Then, one day, I came across Harold Kushner's book, *When Bad Things Happen to Good People*. This brave rabbi had faced my dilemma head-on and had decided to make a judgment call. He was able to accept a God who was all good but not all powerful, but not a God who was all powerful but not all good. The book not only had made a huge stir in theological seminaries, but also had found a wide readership among ordinary people of all faiths, including me.

In my case, I decided no longer to blame God for the death of my grandparents. Since God gave us free will and therefore chose not to exercise some of his power, it clearly followed that the Nazis, not God, were to be held accountable for the Holocaust. This, in turn, led me to another insight: if God was not all powerful he needed help—from *all* of us, if possible. This made life a test between an active Good and an active Evil in which we were free to choose sides. I found this insight liberating, in fact, exhilarating, because I could reconcile it with my reason.

When it came to religion in general, I came to believe that it was more important *how* one believed than *what* one believed. If one exercised one's belief with respect and acceptance for the beliefs of others, one was likely to contribute to the sum total of good in the world. If, however, one believed that one's own belief was the only way to salvation, then one would no doubt contribute to the sum total of human suffering.

On a recent journey to Jerusalem, I visited Yad Vashem, the Holocaust museum. I left it overwhelmed and crushed. As I came out, however, there was the Avenue of the Righteous, lined with hundreds of trees planted to honor the non-Jews who had risked their lives to help the Jewish people in their despair. My own life had been saved four times through the selflessness and generosity of four strangers who put their lives at risk to save my own. Hence, in my case, absolute good had prevailed over absolute evil. I was a youngster then, and a very lucky one indeed.

There is a far more compelling example than my own, however, that illuminates this truth. During the years of the Nazi Reich,

Adolf Hitler was the only person who ever addressed the Austrian people from the balcony of the Heldenplatz in Vienna. It was his favorite venue from which to deliver his anti-Semitic diatribes. More than half a century later, however, with Hitler long dead and gone, the only other person chosen by the Austrian people to speak to them from that particular balcony was my friend Elie Wiesel, survivor of Auschwitz. Millions of people watched this event. This was not justice, however; there was none for the six million Jews who had been murdered by the Nazis. But a man of peace, recognized as such the world over, did have the last word after all.

CHAPTER 13

Vienna, 2010

Never, since that terrible year 1938, did I ever expect to see Vienna again, and yet fate had decreed that I would. The story of this visit, which took place in March 2010, exactly seventy years after I had left Austria as a ten-year-old boy, constitutes a fitting mention.

In January 2010, I received a surprising letter from an Austrian organization that described itself as the Jewish Welcome Service. I was invited to visit Vienna as a member of a small group of Holocaust survivors and was asked whether I was willing to address a large number of Austrian parliamentarians in the Hofburg Palace on my reflections on the Holocaust and its meaning in history. The Holocaust group also included my childhood friend Susi, who had been a member of the Kindertransport and who had barely escaped into the arms of total strangers in Wales. The memory of the terrible scene of Susi's mother, Trudy, who ran screaming after the train as it pulled out of the railroad station, came back to me.

Jewish Welcome Service? I wondered. The phrase struck me as a prize oxymoron as I thought back to my own memories of 1938 when Lisl and I stood on the Ringstrasse, watching Adolf Hitler's triumphant arrival in a Vienna decked out with thousands of swastika flags.

I decided to call the sender of the letter and was pleasantly surprised with the response and information I received. When I asked him whether the Austrians were finally ready to accept the truth that they had been complicit in Hitler's annexation of their country and that the portrait of Austria as Hitler's "first victim" was an outright lie, the man not only agreed, but also encouraged me. The only path to reconciliation between Austria and the rapidly dwindling number of Holocaust survivors, he said, was to at long last tell the truth. And so it came about that, on the morning of March 12, 2010, I flew to New York to board a plane for Vienna. I arrived there the next day.

As a car marked JEWISH WELCOME SERVICE drove me into downtown Vienna, the first thing I noticed was how little the city had changed over the decades. With a pang of recognition, I passed the very spot on the Ringstrasse where Lisl and I had stood a lifetime ago to await the Fuehrer. The tramways and trolleys I had been forbidden to ride were still running and even bore the same numbers. I was deposited at a comfortable hotel where I was reunited with Susi, who had flown in from North Carolina. We were welcomed by a pleasant couple, Gaston and Elizabeth Mariotti, who assigned us each a room and then reimbursed us for our expenses. The entire group of about thirty people was then asked to board a chartered bus for the ride to the Hofburg, where we would be officially welcomed by the president of Austria, Dr. Heinz Fischer.

The Hofburg was situated among the sumptuous surroundings of Schönbrunn Palace, the seat of the old Habsburg Empire that had ruled over both Austria and Hungary. Dr. Fischer's address was another pleasant surprise. The Austrian president evoked the events of 1938 and spoke movingly of Dr. Kurt von Schuschnigg, the then-president of Austria, a devout Catholic who, in March 1938, had decided not to challenge the German army as it crossed the border into Austria, and who had delivered a farewell message on the radio with the words "God Protect Austria." I remembered him as the tragic figure I had met at St. Louis University in the 1960s, serving as an adjunct professor of international law, who had returned to die in his native Austria, a broken man who had never forgiven himself. Dr. Fischer then announced that the Jewish Welcome Service had been created to show the new Austria to the Holocaust survivors, invited to make up their own minds whether reconciliation was in the realm of the possible.

The next few days were a whirlwind of activity. I was most interested in the younger generation and how they felt about the Hitler years. To my amazement, I discovered that the history of the Holocaust was being taught in all Austrian schools and that Holocaust deniers were punished by jail sentences. I attended a spontaneous student demonstration on the Heldenplatz where Hitler had delivered one of his rabidly anti-Semitic speeches seventy years earlier. Hundreds of students had gathered there and had lit candles in honor of the Holocaust victims. I interviewed dozens of them and they all responded with sincerity that the time was long overdue for admitting that Austria had not been a victim but had been an active participant in the crimes of the Holocaust. I spoke to numerous government officials and parliamentarians who assured me that Austria was now a vibrant democracy and an active and respected member of the European Union. Certainly, they readily admitted, there were occasional extreme right-wing outbursts, but these were relegated to the lunatic fringe. The most impressive thing about the new Austria, I learned, was its total commitment to the concept that the price of membership in the European Union was the renunciation of war as an instrument of national policy. Young men were permitted and encouraged to substitute *Gedenkdienst*, a civilian service dedicated to preserving the lessons of the Holocaust, for their year of military service. They were told to help and take care of elderly people who had been victimized by the Nazis in countries they had occupied during the Second World War. I was so impressed by the *Gedenkdienst* concept that I befriended a number of young people with whom I intended to stay in touch.

There were lighter moments as well. The group was bussed to Grinzing in the Vienna Woods to partake of new wine and good food at one of its famed restaurants. Since I was not much of a wine drinker, I separated from the group and walked a mile or so to Heiligenstadt, a suburb of Vienna, where Beethoven had lived and where he had written his last will and testament. I found the Beethoven-Haus without much trouble, but alas, it was closed since it was later than eight o'clock, the closing hour. However, seeing a light in a window above my head, I decided to be persistent and knocked at the door. When there wasn't an answer, I banged on it. Suddenly, the window above me opened and an elderly lady peeked out and asked gruffly in an unmistakable Viennese accent, "What the hell do you want?" I meekly responded that I was an American tourist who wished to purchase a copy of Beethoven's testament. She disappeared for a moment and then I saw a little basket descending on a string from her window, reminding me of Rumpelstilzchen. In the basket was a copy of the testament.

"Send up five euros!" the old lady demanded.

"I am out of euros," I said plaintively. "May I send you dollars?"

"I don't want dollars," she yelled back at me. "I want euros!" I waved up a twenty-dollar bill in a last desperate effort.

"*Gut,*" she said, apparently satisfied with the deal as I sent up the unpopular American currency.

"Yes," I mused, "the euro is worth more now than the American dollar."

I then walked to the Beethovengang, where the composer had conceived the "Pastoral Symphony" at a time when he could still hear the chirp of the birds and the sound of the wind in the trees. I couldn't help but think of the incredible courage it must have taken to turn away from suicide and to compose the Ninth Symphony, culminating in the "Ode to Joy," the melody of which had been adapted for the anthem of the European Union.

When the final day of our trip arrived, we were summoned once again to the Hofburg. I had been appointed by the little group to be its spokesman. There was an overflow audience, including the president of Austria.

"No one could have imagined in 1938 the Austria of 2010," I began. "It's almost like a miracle. Never take it for granted; cherish it. You are helping to free Europe from the scourge of war. With your help, twenty-six countries have sworn to give up war. Europe today is the first continent that is almost free of war. The Old World is now the teacher of the New. My home is in America, but I am glad and grateful that I came here.

"We should celebrate this!" I then concluded. "I will sing for you Beethoven's 'Ode to Joy.'"

And I did, the crowd then singing it with me for an encore. There were cheers and tears and fond farewells. It was a memorable event I will never forget.

After my return to the United States, I received dozens of emails, mostly from younger people whom I had met during my visit and with whom I intended to stay in touch. As I began to place my visit in perspective, it occurred to me that the new Austria was a reaction to the old. Hitler had involved Austria in the most terrible crime in history, the Holocaust. Its absolute evil had turned the younger generation away from the horrors of war and all this had occurred in the span of a single lifetime—my own.

So the circle had closed. I was no longer haunted by the memory of Adolf Hitler and an adoring Lisl. I thought of the new Austria and perceived a parallel with my own life. I had dedicated myself to teaching and writing about war and I had discovered that no leader in the twentieth century who began a war came out a winner. It was almost like a morality play. If you start a war, you will lose in the end. I see no reason to change this rule about the events of the early twenty-first century. I believe that humanity can learn to give up its bad habits. We did it with slavery, which, for many centuries, was considered as an integral part of the human condition. It wasn't. We must now learn the same lesson about war.

CHAPTER 14

California, 2011

Around Christmastime, I received a phone call from Joseph Jedeikin, an old friend of mine from Shanghai. We both had attended a British public school there, which had been taken over by the Japanese shortly after they had attacked Pearl Harbor and occupied Shanghai. A Japanese headmaster had assumed control of the school in 1941, and the British teachers were subsequently sent to detention centers. The Japanese language was then added to the teaching curriculum and English and French were taught by teachers from neutral countries. Joe reminded me on the phone that we had taken the same class in literature and that he had admired me because I knew the famous soliloquy "To be or not to be" from Shakespeare's *Hamlet* by heart. I reminded him that he had protected me against a vicious classmate who took enormous pleasure from beating me until I was black and blue.

The reason for his call, Joe explained, was to invite me to a party he was giving on the occasion of his eighty-fifth birthday at his home in San Francisco. He was also inviting the other "Old Shanghai Hands" and mentioned that this would be an opportunity for me to reconnect with old friends I had left behind in 1947.

I did not know Joe very well back then because he was a year older and a class ahead of me in Shanghai. It was only in our seventies that we met, by coincidence, when he visited San Diego on a business trip. Yet, I was eager to accept his invitation because, after his San Diego visit, we had become "phone pals" and made it a habit to converse about our favorite topic: the women we had loved. We were very open with one another and had discovered that there was a profound difference between friendship and love. Friendship does not judge and allows for differences; love does not. I benefited greatly from these conversations and looked forward to seeing Joe again in person.

The reunion in San Francisco on January 4, 2012, was a great success. I discovered that Joe was the head of a very large family who lived all over the world, but who had come to San Francisco to help him celebrate his eighty-fifth birthday. Joe himself was a successful attorney and partner in a well-known law firm. He had made the decision to retire on his birthday and to concentrate on regaining his health from a heart attack and surgery. We saw each other every day of that precious week I spent in San Francisco. We toured the beautiful city, especially Chinatown, which reawakened memories of our years in China.

I found out that Joe had been born in Kobe, Japan. His parents took him to Switzerland, where they spent the first year of World War II. Joe's father owned a watch business in Zurich and did a brisk business selling watch movements to the Japanese. He spoke fluent Japanese and this enabled him to persuade a Japanese Army colonel to exempt him and his family from having to move to the Jewish ghetto in Shanghai in 1943.

Joe's father, I learned, was Latvian, and the fact that he took his family from Switzerland to Shanghai saved their lives. They barely escaped death, since the Latvians collaborated with the Nazis during the war. As bearers of Latvian passports, they probably would have been doomed.

Joe mentioned to me that he visited Riga, the Latvian capital, after the war, and said the Kaddish—the Jewish prayer for the dead—in front of a memorial that had been erected to honor the thousands of Jews who had been murdered in Latvia. He and his family had reached Shanghai as refugees in 1940, one year earlier than I. We had both escaped Hitler's gas chambers in the nick of time.

Not coincidentally, there was another guest at Joe's birthday party. Isaiah Zimmerman, who had also fled from Europe just in time, had become a brilliant psychologist. He was now in great demand by the United States government for consultations concerning American immigration policy.

My one regret was that my dear friend Rusty was unable to participate, because his wife was not well enough to travel the long distance from Australia. I was the only one at Joe's party who had chosen a career in the world of academe. But I felt very much at home with Joe and his family and friends; it was difficult to part with them.

On my last day in San Francisco, I toasted Joe and everyone at his birthday party and sang them Beethoven's "Ode to Joy," the chorale melody from his Ninth Symphony. It was appropriate for that joyful occasion.

It took another year after Joe Jedeikin's birthday party in San Francisco before I was able to reunite with Rusty. His mother's prediction had turned out to be correct: he had left Shanghai for Australia six months after I left for the United States. In Australia, he was obliged to work on building roads for two years and was able to save a tidy sum of money. He also fell in love with an Australian woman named Eve, whom he married. By the time we met again, the couple had children and grandchildren who lived in the United States, near New York City, in a little town in Westchester named Bedford.

In August 2012, Rusty invited me by email to spend a week with him and his family in Bedford. So it came about that I saw Rusty again as the head of a wonderful family: his wife Eve, with whom he celebrated their sixtieth wedding anniversary, and his beautiful daughter Sue and her husband Martin, who held the position of chief financial officer of IBM Worldwide. All of this was in addition to three lively grandchildren with whom "Granddad Rusty" played Scrabble for hours on end. Oh, did we reminisce on the porch of their elegant colonial house! And what a bear hug when we had to part again! Neither one of us could say good-bye. Instead, we said, "See you again soon."

My survival in Shanghai with Rusty was long, long ago. As I look with some reflection in these late years of my life, I believe that Shanghai not only saved our lives, but also made us citizens of the world. If need be, we could survive anywhere. I chose the United States of America, because of its commitment to freedom.

The two pillars of my life have been love and work. I worked hard for the things money could buy, but I worked even harder for the things it couldn't. It was, and still is, my hope to leave behind a spiritual legacy by making a modest contribution to humanity's struggle toward the abandonment of war.